AFROPOP!

AFROPOP!

AN ILLUSTRATED GUIDE TO CONTEMPORARY AFRICAN MUSIC

SEAN BARLOW & BANNING EYRE
WITH JACK VARTOOGIAN PHOTOGRAPHS

CHARTWELL
BOOKS, INC.

Published by
CHARTWELL BOOKS, INC.
A division of BOOK SALES, INC.
114, Northfield Avenue
Edison, New Jersey 08837

A *Saraband* Book

ISBN 0-7858-0443-9

Printed in China

10 9 8 7 6 5 4 3 2 1

The publisher gratefully acknowledges the permission of the
photographers, record companies and individuals listed below
to reproduce photos, and cassette and CD covers in this book
on the pages listed. Every effort has been made to credit the
copyright holders accurately in each case, and to include pho-
tographer credits where provided for publicity material. If any
errors or omissions have occurred, please contact the publisher
so that corrections can be made for future editions:

Sean Barlow: VIII (right), 26 (below), 32, 69 (below); **Banning
Eyre:** VII, 11, 21 (top), 22 (top), 26 (top), 38 (all), 39; courtesy, **Gafaïti Productions:** 55 (left), 60 (top); courtesy, **Globestyle,
UK:** 33 (top left & below); courtesy, **Werner Graebner:** 33 (top
right), 34 (top), 35 (top-artwork by DBC Ringo Arts), 35
(below), 36 (top), 37 (both); courtesy, **Istikhara Music:** 57
(top-Americana, Egypt; left-Delta, Egypt), 58 (top), 62 (left);
© **Jak Kilby:** 12, 15 (below left & right), 20 (below), 25 (below),
26 (below), 42 (below), 45 (below), 46 (both), 51 (below),
58 (below), 60 (below), 65 (top); courtesy, **Rampant Records:**
15 (top-photography David Dodds & Marek Patzer); courtesy,
Rounder Records: 25 (top-photo courtesy of Discosette); courtesy, **Shanachie:** 23 (top-photography Paul Hostetter), 56
(below); courtesy, **Sonodisc, Paris:** 28 (top right), 45 (top),
45 (center-photo Philippe le Roux); courtesy, **Stern's**
(Earthworks/US/UK): 14 (bottom-photography Trevor
Herman/Franco Esposito); courtesy, **Teal:** p16 (top-photography Dion Cuyler)

Special thanks to **Baaba Maal** for giving his permission to appear
on the front cover.

Page 1: Dancer enjoying soukous
Page 2: Ladysmith Black Mambazo
Page 3: (left to right): Oumou Sangare, Les Têtes Brûlées, Thomas Mapfumo
Above: Kanda Bongo Man and his band performing at New York City's Central
Park SummerStage

CONTENTS

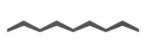

WEST AFRICA

CAMEROON
Frances Bebey
Dina Bell
Moni Bilé
Ekambi Brillant
Georges Collinet
Ben Decca
Manu Dibango
Hoigen Ekwalla
Prince Ndedi Eyango
Toto Guillaume
Sallé John
Guy Lobé
Eboa Lotin
Lapiro de Mbanga
Charlotte Mbango
Vincent Nguini
Les Têtes Brûlées
Sam Fan Thomas
Alaji Toure
Les Vétérans

NIGERIA
King Sunny Ade
Kollington Ayinla
Adewale Ayuba
Sikuru Ayinde Barrister
I.K. Dairo, MBE
Oliver de Coque
Majek Fashek
Haruna Ishola
Ras Kimono
Fela Anikulapo-Kuti
Wasiu Ayinde Marshal
Prince Nico Mbarga
Ebenezer Obey
Sonny Okosuns
Oriental Brothers
Chief Stephen Osita
    Osadabe
Orlando Owoh
Shina Peters
Dele Taiwo

GHANA
Jewel Ackah
Nana Arnpadu & African
    Brothers
Kojo Antwi
A.B. Crentsil
George Darko
Amakye Dede
Dr. K. Gyasi
Daddy Lumba
E.T. Mensah
Koo Nimo
Osibisa
Ramblers International
Carlos Sekyi
Sweet Talks
Tagoe Sisters
Pat Thomas
Nana Tuffour
Western Diamonds

IVORY COAST
Nyanka Bell
Alpha Blondy
Gadji Celi
Emesto Djedje
Gnaoré Djimi
Serge Kasi
Aicha Kone
Sery Simplice
Le Zagazougou
Meiway

SIERRA LEONE
Afro-National
Bosco Banks
Ebenezer Calender &
    Maringar Band
SE Rogie
Abdul T-Jay

GUINEA BISSAU
Kaba Mane
Ramiro Naka
Tino Trimó

TOGO
Itadi K. Bonney
Bessoso

BENIN
Angelique Kidjo
Gnonnas Pedro
Stan Tohon

GUINEA
Camara Aboubacar
Les Amazones

Bala & Ses Balladins
Bembeya Jazz National
Sofa Camayenne
Ibro Diabate
Sekou Bembeya Diabate
Sekouba Bambino Diabate
Sona Diabate
Oumou Dioubate
Kerfala Kante
Mory Kante
Sekou Kandia Kouyate
Ousmane Kouyate
Kante Manfila
Momo "Wandel" Soumah
Keletigui Traore

SENEGAL
Kine Lam
Madou Diabate
Lemzo Diamono
Souleymane Faye
Touré Kunda
Cheikh Lô
Ismael Lô
Baaba Maal
Thio Mbaye

Youssou N'Dour
Orchestra Baobab
Omar Pene
Dudu N'Diaye Rose
Thione Seck
Coumba Gawlo Seck
Mansour Seck

GAMBIA
Foday Musa Suso
Super Eagles
Ifang Bondi
Alhaji Bai Kante
Dembo Kante

MALI
Nanou Coul
Abdoulaye Diabate
Toumani Diabate
Djeneba Diakite
Nahawa Doumbia
Salif Keita
Ami Koita
Sadio Kouyate
Kasse Mady
Fissa Maiga
Rail Band
Oumou Sangare
Dieneba Seck
Coumba Sidibe
Sali Sidibe
Hadja Soumano
Super Biton
Ali Farka Toure
Lobi Traore

GABON
Pierre Akendengue
Les Diablotins
Aziz Inanga
Francois N'gwa

CAPE VERDE
Cesaria Evora
Finaçon
Os Tubaroes
Mindel Band
Mirri Lobo
Tam Tam 2000

NIGER
Saadou Bori
Moussa Poussy

NORTH AFRICA

MOROCCO
Najat Aatabou
Aisha Kandisha's Jarring Effects
Mustapha Baqbou
Bouchebcheb
Bachir Attar & Master Musicians
    of Joujouka
Hassan Erraji
Jil Jilala
Gnawa Halwa
Lem Chaheb
Nass El-Ghiwane
Hassan Hakmoun

ALGERIA
Houria Aicha
Safy Boutella
Djur Djura

Fadela
Zahouania
Cheb Nasro
Cheb Mami
Sahraoui
Cheikha Remitti
Hasni
Khaled
Bellemou Messaoud

SUDAN
Hamza el Din
Muhamed Gubara
Abdel Aziz el Mubarak
Abdel Gadir Salim
Mohamed Wardi

CHAD
Clement Masdongar

EGYPT
Ahmed Adaweyah
Khaled Agag
Amr Dieb
Abd el-Halim Hafez
Hanan
Oum Kalsoum
Ali Hassan Kuban
Mohamed Mounir
Shabaan Abdu Raheem
Salamat
Fathy Salama & Sharkiat
Abdel Wahab

MAURITANIA
Dimi Mint Abba

TUNISIA
Amina

ETHIOPIA
Wabi Abdrehman
Abyssinia Band
Mahmoud Ahmed
Aster Aweke
Mohammed Awel
Neway Debebe
Tlahoun Gessesse
Alemayehu Eshete
Ethio Stars
Netsanet Mellesse
Roha Band
Kuku Sebiebe
Hebiste Tiruneh
Tukut Band
Walias Band

CENTRAL AND EASTERN AFRICA

TANZANIA
Black Star Musical Club
Culture Musical Club
Juwata Jazz
Maquis Original
Mlimani Park Orchestra
Remmy Ongala
TOT Taarab
Muungano Taarab
Siti bint Saad
Vijana Jazz

CONGO
Essous
Les Bantous de la Capitale
Kosmos
Aurlus Mabele & Loketo
Youlou Mabiata
Pamelo Mounka
Tchico Tchicaya
Zao

ZAIRE
Mbilia Bel
Choc Stars
Diblo Dibala
Franco
4 Stars
Joseph Kabasele (Grand Kallé)
Pepé Kallé
Kanda Bongo Man
Nouvelle Generation
Doctor Nico
Ray Lema
Tabu Ley Rochereau
M'Pongo Love
Sam Mangwana
Tshala Muana
Koffi Olomide
Soukous Stars
Papa Wemba
Wenge Musica
Zaiko Langa Langa

KENYA
Joseph Kamaru
Peter Kigia
Maulidi & Musical Party
Collela Mazee & Victoria Kings
Counsilor DK
D.O. Misiani & Shirati Jazz
Kapere Jazz Band
Katitu Boys
Les Wanyika
George Mukabi
Peter Mwambi & Kyanganga
    Boys
Gabriel Omolo
Sukuma Bin Ongaro
Simba Wanyika
Shem Tube & Abana Ba Nasery
Virunga
Zein Musical Party

UGANDA
AFRIGO Band
Ayub Ogada
Geoffrey Oryema
Samite

MALAWI
Alick Nkhata
Kasambwe Brothers

RWANDA
Cécile Kayirebwa

SOUTHERN AFRICA

SOUTH AFICA
Afican Jazz Pioneers
Thomas Chauke & Sinyori
    Sisters
Chicco
Yvonne Chaka-Chaka
Johnny Clegg & Savuka
Dark City Sisters
Lucky Dube
Ihashi Elimhlope
Izintombi Zesi Manje Manje
Brenda Fassie
Abdullah Ibrahim
Sipho Mabuse
Jabu Khanyile & Bayete
Ladysmith Black Mambazo
Mahlathini & Mahotella
    Queens
Miriam Makeba
Hugh Masekela
Spokes Mashiyane

Vusi Mahlasela
Mzwakhe Mbuli
Obed Ngobeni & Kurhula
    Sisters
Ray Phiri & Stimela
Soul Brothers
Tananas
Vusi Ximba

ZIMBABWE
Robson Banda
Bhundu Boys
Black Umfolosi
Blackites
John Chibadura
Stella Rambisai Chiweshe
Leonard Dembo
Four Brothers
Ketai & Simba Brothers
Legal Lions
Lovemore Majaivana
Thomas Mapfumo

Dorothy Masuka
Jonah Moyo & Devera Ngwena
Ephat Mujuru
Oliver Mutukudzi
John Pounds
Shangara Jive

MOZAMBIQUE
Eduardo Durao
Eyuphuru
Ghorwane
Marabenta Star
Orchestre Marabenta
Mil Quinhento

MADAGASCAR
Mily Clément
D'Gary
Roger Georges
Ejema
Jean Emilien
Jaojoby Eusebe

Dama Mahaleo
Ricky
Rossy
Tarika
Tarika Sammy
Zaza Club

ZAMBIA
Amayenge
Bwaluka Founders
Mashabe
Shalawambe

ANGOLA
Valdamar Bastos
Paulo Flores
Kafala Brothers
Bonga
Filipe Mukenga
Eduardo Paim
Orchestra Os Jovens do Prenda
Ruka Vandunen

THE AFROPOP CONVERSATION

Afropop encompasses the end-lessly creative conversation between instruments and play-ers, singers and their fans, the village and the city, the living and their ancestors, between generations and chang-ing attitudes, local roots and the interna-tional pop culture.

By "Afropop", we mean the immense and richly varied landscape of contemporary African music. The term does not refer to any one type of music, but to the diverse styles of a whole continent. The purpose of this book is to introduce you to the leading African recording artists and point you to what we consider to be their best work. In *Afropop!*, we profile artists who have had major impact, touching their people deeply in their times; these are artists whose record-ings, for the most part, you can find outside the continent of Africa.

Over the course of the last ten years of making the AFROPOP and AFROPOP WORLDWIDE series for National Public Radio and writing features for publications, we have participated in extraordinary musi-cal events. In an open-air Zairean club, fash-ionably dressed youths shuffle right, shuffle left, and breaststroke twice—picking up new moves from the front four singer-dancers of Zaiko Langa Langa. In Conakry,

Boy playing njarka in Mali

Guinea's smoky, dimly lit Club Bembeya, guitarist Sekou "Diamond Fingers" Diabate charges up the scale, releasing a rush of bright searing sound that cuts through the horns and drums and the silvery circling patterns of the rhythm guitarist, leaving a note missing at the top, silent, before his manic dive and the crowd's ecstatic roar. In a suburb of Harare, Zimbabwe, neighbors gather in the evening to drink local African beer and dance to **mbira** music until cele-brants become possessed with the spirits of ancestors. And we've had the honor of being welcomed into the homes of many of the greats of African music—Youssou N'Dour in Senegal, Ami Koita in Mali, Franco and Tabu Ley in Zaire, and Mahlathini in South Africa, to name a few. We are pleased to pass their stories on to you.

A TWO-WAY STREET

The Afropop conversation links leading African musicians to a growing worldwide network of fans, and the media and music industries ever on the lookout for new opportunities. In the '60s and '70s, path-breaking African artists such as Miriam Makeba and Manu Dibango enjoyed surprise hits. Miriam's "Click Song" and Manu's "Soul Makossa" proved more than catchy tunes; they put names and faces on what remained a largely undifferentiated continent for most westerners. Now, the conversation has inten-sified as dozens of African recording artists release albums and tour internationally— Senegalese superstars Youssou N'Dour and Baaba Maal, Mali's Salif Keita, Algeria's *rai* king Khaled, Zaire's top **soukous** dance bands, South Africa's Ladysmith Black Mambazo, and many more. These stars are opening ears to the singers and bands that have thrilled local audiences for decades, including many who have not yet performed abroad but whose recordings are now available.

Franco, the giant of Zairean music with hundreds of releases to his credit, sat with us in the courtyard of his compound in Kinshasa in 1985, and recalled how he and his contemporaries used to listen to Otis Redding, Aretha Franklin and James Brown, even though they could not understand the words. Then he said with a hard edge in his voice, "We know your music. Why don't you know ours?" Good question. The fact is there

has been an active recording industry in Africa since the turn of the century. And some powerhouse styles, like Ghanaian *high-life* in the '50s and '60s and Congolese *rumba/* Zairean soukous from the '60s to the present, have reached a pan-African audience.

Unfortunately Franco is not here to see more of the two-way street that there's now connecting Africa and the world beyond. The credit, of course, goes to the sheer tal-ent and determination of African recording artists. Major breakthroughs along the way came from Nigerian *juju* maestro King Sunny Adé's landmark tours in Europe and North America in 1982-'83 and Paul Simon's "Graceland" recording and tour in 1986-'87. Important exposure also came from Peter Gabriel's WOMAD organization, and, we are proud to say, National Public Radio's AFROPOP and AFROPOP WORLDWIDE series in the US from 1988 on. Meanwhile, Paris, the crossroads of the French-speaking African world, exploded in the '80s as a major recording and media center for African music. Credit is also due to numerous hardworking independent record labels, concert and festival presenters, fanzines, journal-ists and local radio programmers around the world.

THE LONG CONVERSATION

The conversation between African music and world culture has actually been going on for centuries. Internally, Africans have a long history of building great cultures and empires—Ashanti, Manding, Songhai, Egypt, Kongo, Zulu—and in so doing have conquered neighbors, both spreading and absorbing cultural influences. In the 16th century, the kingdom of Morocco brought Gnawa people from Mali to serve as slaves in the imperial cities, where they became recognized for their skills as musicians and healers. The trans-Atlantic slave trade brought millions of Africans to the Carib-bean and the Americas where, despite brutal conditions, they ingeniously adapted African instruments, lyric themes, and aes-thetic principles, to make creolized New World traditions. So in fact, the major pop

music forms in the Americas—from Afro-Cuban *son*, pan-American *salsa*, Brazilian *samba*, Dominican *merengue*, and Trinidadian *calypso* and *rapso*, to American blues, r&b, rock-and-roll and hip-hop—are profoundly Africanized from their births. Moreover, African musical and aesthetic concepts have influenced everything in the societies they have touched; from language and slang to styles of dance and dress and even the style of radio broadcasting!

First-time listeners often comment that Zairean soukous "sounds Latin." That makes sense, considering that the ancestors of the creators of Afro-Cuban music came largely from West and Central Africa in the first place. And in an Afropop payback, Cuban recordings were widely heard in Africa on the famous "GV" series in the '30s, '40s and '50s which inspired such seminal figures as Franco and Joseph Kabesele in the 1950s colonial capital Leopoldville, the crucible of modern Zairean music later renamed Kinshasa.

Other listeners hear the Grammy-award winning work of Ali Farka Toure from Mali and say it sounds "bluesy". Many of the slaves who were brought to the American south came from West Africa in the first place. Colonists in America firmly discouraged any forms of cultural expression among their slaves, but it stands to reason that old African melodies using the minor pentatonic or blues scale melodies found their way into the mix of American music. Ali Farka Toure certainly thinks so. He asserts

that, whatever others may hear, he is singing from ancient Bambara, Songhai, Peul and Tamasheck sources.

Afropop ping-pong continues to this day, as African musicians listen to Jamaican reggae, Caribbean *zouk*, American hip-hop, and re-Africanize these styles with new interpretations. Likewise, Cuban, Brazilian and Haitian musicians today look directly to the Yoruba pantheon of gods and the related culture brought over from West Africa.

THE MUSIC TRADITION

Ghanaian master drummer Abraham Adzenyah advises, "Listen to the bell; the bell is the invisible connector." Chattering around the bell is the conversation between the *kaganu* and the *kidi* drums, between the *axatse* shakers and *sogo* drums, between all the drums and the *atsemazu* master drum, each with its distinctive tonality and texture and rhythmic role to play in the whole. The conversationality of West African drum music is widely echoed in the work of popular recording artists on the continent. Listen to the dialogue between the solo, mi-solo and rhythm guitars in a Zairean soukous band. Check out the passionate exchange between a love-stricken Ethiopian singer and the swooning saxophone that mirrors his pain.

The focus of *Afropop!* is on urban electric African pop music played by professional musicians, but many of these musicians have come to the city from the countryside. And they transform their village music to the urban pop palette—electric guitars, horns, keyboards and trap drums. For example, Zimbabwe's Thomas Mapfumo, along with his many collaborators, adapted the ancient *mbira*, or thumb piano, music of his Shona people to guitars and trap drums. Pop artists throughout much of North Africa prominently feature keyboards in their sound because, in part, they can tune them to traditional scales, thus preserving an ancient feeling in aggressively modern music. So the amazing variety of instruments in Africa—drums, reeds, flutes, tuned percussion, stringed instruments, both plucked and bowed—live on in new contexts. At the same time, village traditions still go on in a living continuum where the collective genius of a group is more celebrated than individual stardom.

Besides the instruments, the rhythms from the village are refreshingly different from the straight-ahead 4/4 of most international pop music. The three-against-two feel of 6/8 time, filtered out of many of African music's descendants in the west, emerges strongly in

some of the continent's contemporary pop forms including Cameroonian *bikutsi*, Malagasy *salegy*, Zimbabwean *mbira pop* and Ivorian *polihet*.

Francis Bebey, the Cameroonian multi-instrumentalist, composer and author says, "The dead are never dead." Music has always played a key role in the conversation between the living and the ancestors in Africa. The ancestors provide guidance and spiritual healing to those on earth in ceremonies where music helps open the channels of communication. Some of this music turns the dance floor into a high mass, where communication with the ancestors enriches the mood of celebration.

VOICES RAISED AND HEARD

Too often, Africa gets depicted in the press as a lost cause, a place where nothing works. Any honest observer must see the persistent problems—colonially-drawn boundaries that divide once unified societies, corrup-

tion, lack of institutions, and poverty. But many African governments are moving toward democracy, independent media and more open economies. For a long time, African journalists and intellectuals have been suppressed by the state and the role of social observer and commentator, always important for musicians in Africa, has been amplified. Fela Kuti scathingly satired military rule in Nigeria in such songs as "Zombie," which was answered with vicious attacks by the army. Singer Mohamed Wardi, from the dominant north in Sudan, reached across one of most bitterly contested ethnic and cultural divides on the continent by going to perform for cheering refugees of a vanquished southern rebel cause. In many cases, musicians have worked in slyer ways to comment indirectly. The use of animal parables and old proverbs is a favorite technique. Still, some songs prove too transparent; in Ghana, "The Driver is Different, But the Lory is the Same" got banned by the authorities.

Music in Africa has always been tied to moral commentary and social observation, both serious and humorous. For African pop musicians, that's part of their conversation with their fans. Franco loved to comment on relations between men and women such as in his mid-'80s megahit, "Mario," about a gigolo down on his luck. The young Oumou Sangare from Mali questions the common practices of arranged marriages and polygamy. Khaled, now exiled from Algeria, led a generational revolt in the '80s against conservative social norms and celebrated the pleasures of romance and drink. The South African reggae star Lucky Dube, performed his megahit "Slave," ostensibly about alcohol, in the bad old days of apartheid for throngs of black township teenagers. When Lucky asked his fans to raise their hands if they were slaves, they did so in a heartbreaking testimony to their predicament.

The African tradition of signifying in song—either directly or indirectly—individual and collective foibles and failings lives on in New World music genres. Trinidadian calypso, Brazilian samba, Jamaican reggae, and American hip-hop all take on topical issues with wit and gusto.

THE LONG ROAD
The conversation between Afropop and the international music and media industries raises particularly thorny issues. Musicians in cash-poor African countries are often dependent on local clubowners and cassette producers to provide them with access to tools of their trade—instruments, PA systems, recording equipment. As artists grow more successful and more in control, they face new challenges—international record companies and promoters—as well as artistic dilemmas. The urge for wider recognition—the dream of a worldwide audience— may encourage musicians to do things that displease the home crowd. Similarly, keeping the home crowd happy may involve choices that turn off listeners from outside.

A western listener might be puzzled hearing musicians from percussion-rich countries such as Ghana and Nigeria use programmed drum sounds. It may simply be a producer's strategy for getting clean sound or saving money. But for African

musicians, that choice might represent a triumphant embrace of modernity, and one that the home audience demands categorically. There are no "right" or "wrong" answers, only choices that particular listeners like or dislike depending on their taste and point of view. And purism does not really belong in any discussion about pop music whose essence is to grow, absorb and change.

Senegalese superstar Baaba Maal, pictured on the cover, expresses with characteristic insight the larger challenge for Afropop: "My greatest concern is that African music succeeds in achieving its potential. Africans have a side that is good for mankind—their community, their tolerance, their love of fellow man. African music gives courage to those who live it. We have women going to the well to get water. It's heavy on their heads, but at the same time they smile and sing along the way. Through me and musicians like me, this music can also evolve on the international plane to bring people together. But this can only be done by taking the music into the international show business circuit. This is hard, because the African continent has its own realities, and you have to present the music in its totality, along with the role it plays in each society. You can't close your eyes to others in the end of the 20th century."

SOME NOTES ON THE BOOK
Music lovers around the world are opening their eyes and ears to Africa's musical genius.

However, the outside world is hearing a fraction of what Africa offers. Beyond the stars who have achieved well-deserved international recognition, thousands of popular African musicians record for the booming cassette markets of Cairo, Lagos, Accra, Abidjan, Dakar, Harare, and elsewhere. Their music rarely gets heard outside the continent. We have included selected rosters of these artists if you should be lucky enough to browse a cassette stall in Africa. There are also now cassette import services available (see Sources section). And in your own city, you may very well find tapes in grocery and variety stores run by African émigrés. Introduce yourself. Shake hands with the patrons—it's customary—and ask them to play you some of their favorite music. You are sure to see the smile of Africa.

We make no claim that *Afropop!* is a complete, exhaustive study. Space limitations make that impossible. We apologize to the many talented artists we could not include here. Sometimes even whole countries—Tunisia, Gabon, Uganda, to name some—are not featured. (See the Supplementary Discography which includes music from these countries). While we are at it, we might as well own up to the fact that the truth in this under-researched music is often difficult to establish. Who was the first? Who was the biggest? Who gave a style its name? Sometimes you get a different answer every time you ask the question. There are many artists and musical cultures yet to be written about in depth, and many more compilations of nearly-forgotten musicians from golden musical eras to be made. So don't expect the last word. Do expect that this book will point the way to extraordinary artists and beautiful recordings. And Jack Vartoogian's gorgeous photos will delight you with the visual and visceral excitement of African music performed live.

At whatever point you enter the Afropop conversation, as African musicians are fond of saying, "You are welcome. Music has no frontiers."

Note: We welcome your comments and suggestions for the next edition of *Afropop!*
Send them to:
World Music Productions
328 Flatbush Ave., Suite 288
Brooklyn, NY, USA 11238.
Or you can e-mail us at afropop@npr.org

Opposite, left: Massamba Diop playing tama
Opposite, center: Ad hoc musical gathering in Tamale, Ghana   Above: Papa Wemba from Zaire

SOUTHERN AFRICA

South Africa has given the world some of the most memorable voices from the African continent—the soaring, passionate alto of Miriam Makeba, the purr and pounce of Ladysmith Black Mambazo, the amazing sub-bass groaning of Mahlathini, and many others. Such vocal virtuosity is not surprising coming from a land where, Zulus, Xhosas and Sothos have for centuries celebrated life's large and small moments with song. Many South African artists started out singing in mission school choirs or in church. And when they made the jump to the commercial music world, a sophisticated recording industry awaited them.

South Africa has the most developed recording history on the continent with a prolific local music industry that's been pumping out commercial releases for over a half century. The first commercial recordings were made in South Africa in 1912, and S.A. music industry pioneer Eric Gallo established the first recording studio in the country in the 1930s. The major South African record companies today are Gallo, Teal, Tusk, CCP/EMI and BMG.

THE SA-US CONNECTION

For over a century, South Africa, more than any other African country, has looked to the United States for musical inspiration. The discovery of gold and diamonds in the 19th century created an urban population hungry for entertainment. And travelling African-American minstrel shows, vaudeville acts and gospel groups helped fill the bill, making a big impression on local audiences. American jazz artists and jazz arrangement concepts energized the embryonic South African jazz scene from the '30s on. American soul, disco and hip-hop from the '60s to the present all have their offspring in South Africa.

The following profiles tell the stories of the leading South African recording artists and the varied styles they defined—*South African jazz, kwela, mbaqanga, mbube, neo-traditional,* soul, disco, and reggae. Perhaps it is more accurate to say "S.A. soul", "S.A. disco" and "S.A. reggae" since local artists stamped the styles with a unique South African identity.

Imagine a visitor's surprise on going to major black township festivals in South Africa expecting to hear mbaqanga township jive only to hear band after band playing disco

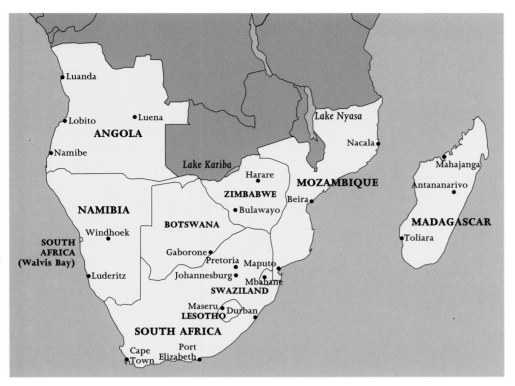

Unlimited. From his start singing covers of western pop hits, Thomas, along with his many collaborators, went on to create a singularly Zimbabwean sound, *chimurenga*, that at once claimed a modern place for ancient Shona music and rallied people during the war for an independent Zimbabwe.

MALAGASY MAGIC

To the east, on the vast Indian Ocean island of Madagascar, forests, beaches, and highland plains support flora and fauna found nowhere else, and 18 ethnic groups, descended from Africans, Arabs, Europeans and Southeat Asians play equally rare music. Star musician and bandleader Rossy says, "Malagasy people are a mixture of Asian and African. The Asian side is sad, bluesy and cool. The coast is hot…the coast is Africa. The mix is fantastic." And indeed Rossy's words are borne out by an impressive array of sounds and artists which became available to the world market only in the last several years. From the coastal *salegy* dance music to the reflective *valiha* music of the central highlands to the raucous street theater and music contests called *hiragassy,* there is much to explore from Madagascar.

Two southern African countries—Angola and Mozambique—have recently emerged from devastating civil wars. Both were belatedly free from Portuguese colonial rule in 1975. Few international releases have emerged from these musically rich countries, and we look forward to what the future brings.

Opposite, above: Mahlathini   Opposite, below: Miriam Makeba with Hugh Masekela   Below: Zimbabwe Landscape

music driven by banks of keyboards. Asking when the mbaqanga will be played draws the laughing reply, "Oh, that was popular in the '70s."

Ironically, many South African sounds that have achieved recognition in the outside world are generally considered passé back home. Musical taste in South Africa has often followed political events. The 1976 student uprising in Soweto was a turning point; the young generation shunned their parents' choices including music and embraced what they thought was the more progessive forms of soul and disco.

Musicians in South Africa now complain that national radio is saturated with American music, leaving little space for local music and they've organized to demand that a mininum quota for local South African content on radio be put in place. It's also true that now that economic sanctions have been lifted, competition from international acts playing South Africa is stiff. However the wealth of musical talent in South Africa, the momentum of the recording industry, and current reassessment of indigenous music will surely yield welcome results.

HARARE'S DANCING

To the north of South Africa, in neighboring Zimbabwe, the weekend nightlife in the capital, Harare, pulsates with guitar bands playing for dancehappy crowds till early in the morning. Fans follow their favorite stars on the circuit from the Kambazumba Garden Party and Job's Nite Spot to Queen's Garden.

Zimbabwe has historically been a sort of musical crossroads between the two regional powerhouses—South Africa and Zaire. Pinched between the overwhelming influences of Zairean *rumba* and *soukous,* and South African jive, as well as British and American pop, Zimbabwean pop groups struggled for identity in the '60s and '70s. The following essays describe some of the most successful creators of popular blends—Jonah Moyo and Devera Ngwena, John Chibadura, James Chimombe, Leonard Dembo.

But the most outstanding artist to emerge from Zimbabwe is Thomas Mapfumo, singer, composer and bandleader of the Blacks

SOUTH AFRICAN JAZZ

In the years following World War I, musicians in South Africa's township slums created the jaunty **marabi** sound, which used piano, and later banjo and guitar, to animate African melodies and cyclic, three-chord progressions. 1930s marabi groups applied jazz band principles to the music, bringing in saxophones and creating the foundation for South Africa's swing era. By the '40s, urban jazz bands like the **Merry Blackbirds**, the **Harlem Swingsters** and the **Jazz Maniacs** covered American swing hits by groups like Count Basie and Glen Miller to delight an emerging middle class. After World War II, gifted horn players **Isaac "Zacks" Nkosi** and **Kippie Moeketsi** helped to develop a more improvisation-oriented sound that supercharged Johannesburg's fledgling jazz scene. Female jazz singers **Dorothy Masuka**, **Miriam Makeba** and **Dolly Rathebe** became stars loved for their glamour as well as their expressive voices. Signaling the end of a rich musical era, apartheid's restrictive Group Areas Act of 1950 closed down venues where whites had been able to go and hear black musicians, and led to the bulldozing of the cultural community known as Sophiatown. But recording continued. In 1960, the **Jazz Epistles**, heavily influenced by American cool jazz, made one of the country's first full-length albums, and their pianist **Dollar Brand** and trumpeter **Hugh Masekela** went on to earn international fame. With the rise of township jive and soul, jazz groups declined in the '70s. More recently though, jazz has made a comeback, signified by the opening of Kippie's, a Johannesburg jazz club. By the early '80s, one veteran bandleader and saxman, **Ntemi Piliso** had pulled together a full-sized horn band, the **African Jazz Pioneers,** who currently record and perform for a surprisingly young audience. Marrying the sunny harmonies and hard swing of old-time jazz with the propulsive drive of **mbaqanga** pop, this band's sound encompasses the diverse flavors and resilient spirit of a unique African jazz legacy.

○ *The African Jazz Pioneers* **Live at Montreux** (KAZ, UK) • **Sip 'N Fly** (Gallo, SA/Flame Tree, UK)
○ *Jonas Gwwangwa,* **Flowers of the Nation** (Kariba/Tusk, SA)
○ *Jazz Epistles,* **Verse One** (Celluloid, France)
○ *Zacks Nkosi,* **A Tribute to Zacks Nkosi** (Gallo, SA/Celluloid, France)
○ *Philip Tabane & Molombo,* **Umh** (Nonesuch, US)
○ *Sipho Gumede,* **Down Freedom Avenue** (B&W, UK)
○ *Various Artists,* **From Marabi to Disco** (Gallo, SA) • **Jazz in Africa, Vols 1-2** (Teal, SA/KAZ, UK) • **Township Swing Jazz, v. 1-2** (Harlequin, US/ Cellluloid, France) • **Jazz and Hot Dance in S. Africa, 1946-49,** (Harlequin, US) • **Drum—South Arican Jazz and Jive, 1954-1960** (Monsun/Line, Germany)

ABDULLAH IBRAHIM

Jazz composer and pianist **Abdullah Ibrahim**, better known as **Dollar Brand,** came to prominence with the **Jazz Epistles** in the early '60s. Like so many successful musicians of that era, he traveled to Europe and US, where he got encouragement from no less a mentor than Duke Ellington. Dollar stayed abroad for 12 years, but then briefly returned to his old stomping grounds in Cape Town where he helped forge a new sound unique to that place. The warm, breezy music that resulted embodied the free spirit of jazz. But at a time when American jazzmen gravitated towards oblique harmonies, and then electric jazz/rock fusion, Dollar Brand and the Cape Town players kept the spirit of '50s cool jazz alive. They gave the music a soothing, spiritual folk element that later influenced a new school of American players, notably Keith Jarrett. In 1974, Dollar's collaboration with tenor saxophonist **Basil Coetzee** yielded Cape Town jazz's defining recording, *Mannenberg*, a wistful meditation on township life. Now based in New York, Abdullah Ibrahim continues to perform and record critically acclaimed works, and to collaborate with top flight American jazz musicians.

○ *African Marketplace,* (Enja, SA) • **African Sun** (KAZ, UK) • **The African Series, v. 1-4** (KAZ, UK) • **Blues for a Hip King** (KAZ, UK) • **Mindif** (Enja) • **The Mountain** (KAZ, UK) • **Tintinyana** (KAZ, UK) • **Voice of Africa** (KAZ, UK)

MIRIAM MAKEBA

Miriam Makeba—"Mama Africa" to many around the world—ranks as South Africa's greatest musical ambassador. Born in 1932, Miriam had weathered the death of her father, a bout with breast cancer, childbirth and the first of five marriages before she turned twenty. From her start in a church choir, Miriam went on to sing professionally under the strong influence of her American idols, Ella Fitzgerald and Sarah Vaughan. Miriam left the popular **Manhattan Brothers** to join the traveling show *African Jazz and Variety*, which toured southern Africa for 18 months. Miriam's superior voice then earned her the lead in the show *King Kong*, and a film part in *Come Back Africa*. Suddenly an international star, Miriam then played at President Kennedy's birthday and worked with Harry Belafonte in New York to create African classics including "The Click Song," and "Pata Pata." After the South African government canceled her passport in 1960, Miriam spent decades in exile living mostly in the US, and then in Guinea, where she retreated for nine years after her marriage to black power activist Stokely Carmichael soured her reputation with mainstream American media and the music industry. Miriam returned to the world stage in 1986 when she joined Paul Simon on the *Graceland* tour. She writes in her autobiography that music helped her wrestle the dangerous *amadlozi* spirits her mother passed on to her. She dedicates her exquisite 1988 album *Sangoma*, rich in tradition, to her mother. After turmoil, tragedy and controversy, Miriam has returned to a free South Africa as a favorite daughter. Her recent work includes a tour and recording session with jazz great Dizzy Gillespie, who died in 1993.

⊙ **Miriam Makeba and the Skylarks, v. 1-2** (Teal, SA/KAZ, UK) • **Sangoma** (Warner Brothers, US) • **Welela** (Mercury/Polygram, US) • **I Shall Sing** (Ésperance/Sonodisc, France) • **Live Au Palais du Peuple de Conakry** (Ésperance/Sonodisc, France)
⊙ Dorothy Masuka, **Hamba Notsokolo** (African Classics/Gallo, SA)

HUGH MASEKELA

Nobody gets around like trumpeter and bandleader **Hugh Masekela**. Born near Johannesburg in 1939, Hugh has traveled the globe and played with Nigeria's **Fela Kuti**, Zaire's **OK Jazz**, the **Crusaders**, **Herb Alpert** and **Paul Simon**, as well as many South African jazz and pop greats. After anti-apartheid activist Father Trevor Huddleston introduced him to the trumpet, Hugh worked his way into the jazz scene, playing alongside trombonist **Jonas Gwangwa**, clarinet and sax man **Kippie Moeketsi** and later the great **Dollar Brand**. A self-styled "young man with a horn," Hugh played the townships with **Father Huddleston's Jazz Band** and then with the **Jazz Dazzlers** doing jazz covers and *mbaqanga*. But fed up with apartheid's drive to curtail black music, Hugh left his place in the **Jazz Epistles** to go into exile in 1961. Harry Belafonte helped him settle in the US as a student, and Hugh set up shop in New York, recording a number of records in the late '60s and early '70s, including his 1968 number one hit, "Grazing in the Grass." In leaner years ahead, Hugh worked with other South Africans, including jive-gone-jazz saxophone luminary **Dudu Pukwana**. Hugh spent six years exploring music in Senegal, Zaire, Guinea, Nigeria and Ghana. In Ghana, Fela Kuti hooked him up with

Hedzolleh Sounds, a highlife fusion band with whom Hugh returned to the US and recorded what some critics consider his best records. In 1980, Hugh joined **Miriam Makeba** to play for 100,000 in Lesotho, and four years later he established a mobile studio in Botswana and recorded *Technobush*, an mbaqanga/funk fusion album featuring the **Soul Brothers**. When controversy stirred around the *Graceland* tour as a violation of the ANC's cultural boycott, Hugh, a participant, defended Paul Simon vigorously. Hugh's 1987 song "Bring Him Back Home" became the theme for Nelson Mandela's world tour following his release from prison in 1992. Hugh now lives in South Africa, though he travels often to perform and record.

⊙ **Hugh Masekela and the Union of South Africa** (TML) • **Introducing Hedzoleh Soundz** (BTS) • **Waiting for the Rain** (Jive, US) • **Techno Bush** (Jive, US) • **Hope** (Triloka Records, US)

MAHLATHINI AND THE MAHOTELLA QUEENS

Perhaps Africa's hardest-driving pop sound, South African *mbaqanga* delivers frisky riffing and plush vocal harmonies over a knockout downbeat. Mbaqanga grew out of two earlier styles. The popular penny-whistle music known as *kwela*, championed by **Spokes Mashiyane,** developed as a vehicle for playing African urban melodies with a swing feeling using instruments near at hand. Then the raucous, rowdy blare of *sax jive* supplanted kwela in the marketplace. In 1965, **Rupert Bopape,** one of South Africa's great black producers, assembled a group of young session musicians—most of them domestic workers from Pretoria— to form the **Makhona Tsohle** ("Jack of all Trades") **Band.** Kicking out township pop with the uplift of sax jive and the force of American r&b, the group's bassist **Joseph Makwela** and guitarist **Marks Mankwane** in particular forged the all-electric sound that would rock the townships for the next decade. Having produced mbaqanga's seminal vocal group the **Dark City Sisters,** Bopape took one of their guest male vocalists, **Mahlathini,** and teamed him with a new female chorus, the **Mahotella Queens.** Mbaqanga—meaning a homemade dumpling cooked in a hurry—then entered its golden age. The bass "groaner", **Simon Nkabinde** earned the name Mahlathini, "bush on his head," as a reference to his aloof, commanding presence, his link with rural traditions and his unbelievably loud, low voice. Rounded out by the sunny, gospel harmonies of the Mahotella Queens, and by their endlessly inventive dance steps, this supergroup became a sensation throughout southern Africa. The Mahotella Queens took an eight-year break to raise families while another group performed and recorded under the same name. In the early '80s though, three of the original Queens rejoined Mahlathini, and the revived group now keeps busy recording and touring internationally. Other top mbaqanga acts include **Izintombi Zesi Manje Manje** and the **Boyoyo Boys.**

⦿ *Mahlathini,* **King of the Groaners** (Stern's Earthworks)
• **The Lion of Soweto** (Stern's Earthworks)
⦿ **Mahlathini & the Mahotella Queens, Paris-Soweto** (Polygram) • **Thokozile** (Stern's Earthworks) • **Mbaqanga** (Verve World, US)
⦿ **Dark City Sisters and the Flying Jazz Queens** (Stern's Earthworks)
⦿ *Various,* **A Taste of the Indestructible Beat of Soweto** (Stern's Earthworks) • **The Indestructible Beat of Soweto, v. 1-5** (Stern's Earthworks)
⦿ *Spokes Mashiyane,* **King Kwela** (Celluloid, France)
⦿ *West Nkosi,* **Rhythm of Healing** (Stern's Earthworks)
⦿ *The Boyoyo Boys,* **Back In Town** (Rounder, US)
⦿ *Izintombi Zesi Manje Manje,* **Isitha Sami Nguwe** (Gallo, SA)

THE SOUL BROTHERS

After the Soweto student uprising of 1976 and its violent suppression, young South Africans stepped up the fight against apartheid. In this context, traditional pop and mbaqanga gave way to music modeled on American soul, and later disco. Soul bands like the **Movers** rarely addressed politics directly, but they rejected the ethnic associations used to divide people under apartheid and embraced the international sound purveyed by the likes of Wilson Pickett and Percy Sledge. Having formed in '74, a group of ex-factory workers called the **Soul Brothers** rose fast in this environment, and they remain one of the country's top-selling bands today. Bassist **Zenzele Mchunu** and the band's first drummer pounded out a familiar jive beat, but keyboard man **Moses Ngwenya** played billowing organ riffs reminiscent of Booker T and the MGs, and led by singer **David Masondo,** the group developed a shimmering, breathy vocal sound that caught on fast and inspired many imitators. After Zenzele died in a car crash in 1985, David and Moses revamped the group as a 13-piece juggernaut featuring five singers with tight dance moves, and three saxophones led by sax jive veteran **Thomas Phale.** Before their first international tour in 1990, the Soul Brothers had sold four million records and they remain the one township jive act to compete with today's disco stars.

⦿ **Jive Explosion** (Stern's Earthworks) • **Xola** (Soul Brothers Records, SA) • **Jump and Jive** (Stern's Earthworks)

RAY PHIRI AND STIMELA

One of South Africa's bolder pop artists, **Chikapa "Ray" Phiri**, grew up in Malawi where his father "Just Now" Phiri cleaned swimming pools and played the local *highlife* music on acoustic guitar. A thin, limber boy, Ray danced in his father's show until the old man lost three fingers in a machine accident, prompting Ray to pick up the guitar. Moving to Johannesburg in the late '60s, Ray got in on the early days of the soul craze playing guitar for the **Cannibals,** whose organ-based sound backed seminal South African soul stars like **Jacob Mpharanyana Radebe.** The Cannibals evolved into Ray's present group **Stimela** by the early '80s. Mixing up jazz, mbaqanga, funk and soul, Stimela started out backing established singers, including a session with **Sipho "Hotstix" Mabuse** destined for stardom himself in the band **Harari**. Ultimately, Ray emerged as the lead arranger, composer and singer for Stimela,

then well on its way to becoming a super-group. Controversial but soul-searching songs like "Highland Drifter" and "Whispers in the Deep" got banned on SABC (South Africa's state-owned radio station), but established Ray as a voice of national conscience. His fluid arrangements fused soul ballads and township jive, often shifting styles within a single song. In 1985, Ray co-arranged and played on **Paul Simon**'s *Graceland* album, and accompanied the subsequent international tour. Since then, Ray has recorded with and without Stimela, preserving a large, loyal following.

Another fusion artist writing his own ticket, singer **Jabu Khanyile** grew up on Johnny Nash and Jimmy Cliff, as well as his own Zulu roots. His band **Bayete** first emerged in the '80s with jazz and reggae flavorings. Matured now, and with a foot solidly in township traditions, Bayete entreats an international audience with their first release on Mango.

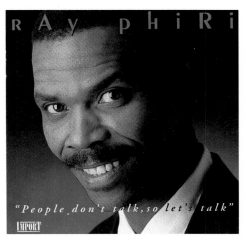

● Ray Phiri & Stimela, **Look Listen and Decide** (Gallo, SA) • **Don't Ask Why** (Gallo, SA)
● Ray Phiri, **People Don't Talk, So Let's Talk** (Rampant, SA)
● Sipho Mabuse, **The Best of Sipho Mabuse** (Gallo, SA)
● Bayete, **Mbombela** (CCP/EMI, SA)
● Bayete & Jabu Khanyile, **Mmalo-We** (Mango, US)

YVONNE CHAKA-CHAKA, BRENDA FASSIE, AND THE RISE OF DISCO

Since the mid-'80s, the keyboard and drum machine-oriented sound called disco, or less flatteringly bubblegum, has ruled the South African townships. The music preserves the pounding downbeat and muscular bass of township jive, but uses straighter grooves and replaces horns, guitars and drums with batteries of synthesizers. Disco's first big star, singer **Yvonne Chaka-Chaka**, burst onto the scene in 1985 with her hit "I'm in Love with a D.J." South African jazz and jive had found audiences throughout southern

Africa, but Yvonne's music traveled further selling 600,000 copies in Nigeria alone, and she soon toured Zaire, Kenya and Nigeria with her band **Taxi**, packing in 70,000 fans in Kinshasa, Zaire. Disco's top seller, **Brenda Fassie** ran away from home at 14 to make her 1970s debut covering the Temptations' "Papa Was a Rolling Stone" with the group **Tiny Tots**. In the '80s, Brenda embraced disco first with the **Big Dudes** and then on her own. Hits like "Weekend Special" and "Good Black Women" led critics to call her the

Madonna of South Africa. Five-foot-one and a dynamo on stage, Brenda plays good time music, but resents the "bubblegum" tag as a highbrow put-down. While other stars have moved into rich, formerly white areas, Brenda still lives near Soweto and peppers her songs with the latest township slang. She feted President Mandela with the song "Black President," and her 1993 album *Amagents* outsold all other South African releases that year. When Brenda got married, 40,000 fans showed up to celebrate.

Left: Yvonne Chaka-Chaka   *Above:* Brenda Fassie

● Yvonne Chaka-Chaka, **The Best of Yvonne Chaka-Chaka** (Teal, SA)
● Brenda Fassie, **Too Late for Mama** (CCP/EMI, SA) • **Black President** (CCP/EMI, SA) • **Yo Baby** (CCP/EMI, SA)

CHICCO

Born in 1963, arranger, producer, singer and instrumentalist **Sello "Chicco" Twala** grew up with music because his father operated an illegal club, or *shebeen*, in Soweto. Rejecting an earlier plan to become a traffic cop, Chicco opened a disco, but then driven by a desire to play music himself, he took up percussion and practiced assiduously to reach a professional level. In the '70s, Chicco played in soul bands including **Umoja** and **Sipho "Hotstix" Mabuse's Harari**. An architect of the disco and bubblegum revolution, Chicco first made a name as a performer in the mid-'80s, but went on to produce major stars, including **Yvonne Chaka-Chaka** and more recently **Brenda and the Big Dudes**. Chicco made his first triple platinum release in 1987, a record that

included the song "We Miss You Manelo," a thinly veiled reference to Nelson Mandela, still a prisoner on Robben Island at the time. In 1990, Chicco collaborated with poet **Mzwakhe Mbuli** on the song "Papa Stop the War." A longtime admirer of music from other parts of Africa, especially Ghana's **Osibisa** and Nigeria's **Fela Kuti**, Chicco then took time off to travel and explore the continent. Chicco's sweet soul ballad "Peace Song," recorded by an all-star South African cast and released in 1992, played an important role in fostering the atmosphere of national unity that preceded South Africa's first democratic election in April 1994. The other major producer of South African disco and bubblegum, **Dan Tshanda**, developed the **Dalom Kids** and **Splash**, bands whose shows feature up to ten keyboards and no other instruments on stage.

- *The Best of Chicco* (Teal, SA) • *Papa Stop the War* (Teal, SA) • *Thina Sizwe* (Teal, SA) • *Soldier Without A Gun* (Philips) • *Chomesa* (Teal, SA)
- Chicco et al, *African Solution* (Tusk, SA)
- Splash, *Greatest Hits* (Gallo, SA)
- Various, *Mpantsula Jive* (Flame Tree, UK)

MZWAKHE MBULI

For years in South Africa, everybody talked about the political situation, but nobody dared sing about it. Nobody, that is, except poet/singer/percussionist **Mzwakhe Mbuli**. Born in the one-time cultural hot spot Sophiatown, Mzwakhe got involved with theater groups after the government bulldozed Sophiatown forcing his

family to move to Soweto. In 1979, his powerful voice earned him the part of God in a play about Job. Inspired by his country's martyrs and prisoners of consciousness—Biko, Mandela and Mambatta, a Zulu chief who resisted the whites to his death—Mzwakhe tried his hand at poetry. In 1981, he read a few of his poems for a funeral crowd and the enthusiastic response he got marked the start of a serious career. Working with the underground Shifty label, Mzwakhe recorded his first record *Change is Pain* in 1987. The government banned the record, forcing Mzwakhe into hiding. The next year, the authorities detained him in solitary confinement for six months, fearing both his message and the power of his performance. But once freed, Mzwakhe continued reciting and performing. Mzwakhe holds forth with a thundering, incantatory voice. Over the jovial swing of classic South African township jive, his cool, breathless oratory takes on the uplift of a gospel revival—like Martin Luther King set to Dixieland jazz. Mzwakhe now fronts his own band and tours internationally. A champion of township styles—*kwela*, *mbaqanga* and jive—Mzwakhe derides local DJ's who he says have "fallen in love with American music." In 1994, Mzwakhe recited at Nelson Mandela's inauguration. Following in Mzwakhe's footsteps, singer **Vusi Mahlasela** now sets political poetry within strong musical arrangements recorded the no-longer-underground Shifty label.

- *Change is Pain* (Rounder, US) • *Resistance is Defence* (Stern's Earthworks) • *Izigi* (CCP/EMI, SA)

TRADITIONAL POP—ZULU, PEDI, SOTHO AND SHANGAAN

Far from the studios and *shebeens* of South Africa's urban centers, rural musicians in Zulu, Sotho, Pedi and Shangaan ethnic enclaves create lively social music. Traditionally strong singers and dancers, the Zulu took a particular shine to two western instruments, guitar and ten-button concertina. The first Zulu concertina records appeared in the '30s, coupling mesmerizing melodic cycles with call-and-response singing. The Zulu's distinctive finger style guitar playing, known as *ukupika*, adapts melodies from various traditional sources, including the ancient mouth bow, to create racing flourishes of notes that settle into insistent, hypnotic grooves, grounded by a heavy downbeat. The typical song arrangement begins and ends with choral singing; in the middle, the singer delivers *ukubonga*, spitfire rapping generally in praise of a clan, family or chief. **John Bhengu** fathered this style in Durban in the '50s and also pioneered the electric version of the music that had great success in rural South Africa during the '70s when artists like **Moses Mchunu, Sipho Mchunu** (pictured at right) and **Kati Elimnyama** produced hundreds of records.

Perhaps the top Zulu traditional pop artist today, **Bheki Ngobo** sings, dances and plays guitar using the stage name **Ihashi Elimhlope** (White Horse). Bheki's music typifies the updated traditional pop sound, lacking the roughness that gave the old groups a measure of their charm, but still packing a hefty punch. After a long lull, the concertina has seen a comeback in recent Zulu pop. Concertina player and singer **Vusi Ximba** found success acting out comic skits with his female dancers in the '70s, and he still records. Vusi's musical comedy release *Siyakudumisa* sold over 100,000 copies in 1993.

The Pedi, an ethnic group closely related to the Sotho, also record using an autoharp in the style called *harepa*. With a beat at least as pounding as the Zulus', Sotho electric groups have evolved from concertina to full-sized accordion and typically favor a gravelly, roaring lead vocal. Sotho groups, such as **Tau Oa Matsheka** and **Tau Ea Linare**, use a six-note scale, rather than western seven-note modes. As an indication of the itinerant nature of these artists, one Sotho singer, **Molahlehi**, "The Lost One," recorded a popular record in 1986, then disappeared. Two years later, the finished record hit the market, but Molahlehi never turned up to claim his glory.

Shangaan groups come from the Northern Transkei region that borders Mozambique, once a Portuguese colony. That proximity led to a Latin flavor in Shangaan music in the '50s, the heyday of singer **Francisco Baloyi.** After 1975 though, the Mozambiquan influence faded when Bantu Radio started an all-Shangaan station. The guitar-based Shangaan sound veers towards rowdy party music, and a faster, lighter groove than the Zulus use. Shangaan groups typically feature a male leader backed by a female chorus, as in the top-ranking **Thomas Chauke and the Sinyori Sisters**, as well as **General MD Shirinda and the Gaza Sisters,** and **Obed Ngobeni and the Kurhula Sisters**, whose song "Kazet No. 2" became a megahit when **Mahlathini and the Mahotella Queens** covered it in 1987.

ZULU

- *Various, **Singing In An Open Space: Zulu Rhythm and Harmony, 1962-1982*** (Rounder, US)
- *Various, **Zulu Jive*** (Rykodisc, US)
- *Ihashi Elimlope, **Ucingo-Telephone*** (Tusk, SA) • **Impendulo** (Tusk, SA)
- *Noise Khanyile, **The Art of Noise*** (GlobeStyle, UK)
- *Mzikayifani Buthelezi, **Fashion Maswedi*** (Rounder, US)
- *Mfiliseni Magubane, **Woza Sihambe*** (Celluloid, US)
- *Amaduduzo, **Siyabamukela*** (Rounder, US)

SHANGAAN / TSONGA

- *Thomas Chauke, **Shimatsatsa*** (series) (Tusk, SA)
- *Obed Ngobeni, **My Wife Bought A Taxi*** (Shanachie, US)
- *Various, **The Heartbeat of Soweto*** (Shanachie, US)

SOTHO

- *Various, **Sheshwe: The Sound of the Mines*** (Rounder, US)
- *Tau Ea Linare, **He O Oe Oe!*** (Globestyle, UK)
- *Tau Ea Matsheka, **Anything you can find*** (CCP/ EMI, SA)

LADYSMITH BLACK MAMBAZO

With roots in the four-part harmony of 19th century African American jubilee singing, Zulu choral music has undergone steady re-Africanization. Nutured in fierce, men's singing competitions in South Africa's mining hostels, the style once known as *mbube* took its name from **Soloman Linda's** big-selling 1939 hit, which the Weavers covered successfully in the US as "Wimoweh" in 1950. The song soared again on the US charts in '61 when the Tokens reworked it as "The Lion Sleeps Tonight." Meanwhile, mbube had evolved into the aggressive, almost shouted 1940s *isikhwela jo*—or "bombing"—and then into the softer, velvety *isicathamiya* ("to walk on one's toes lightly"), pioneered by the **King Star Brothers**. Isicathamiya's most successful popularizers **Ladysmith Black Mambazo** came together in the early '60s under a gentle visionary, **Joseph Shabalala**. Joseph's lithe alto coos and growls above two tenors and seven basses that make soothing, rhythmic textures punctuated by breathy bursts. Joseph's inspiration came in a 1964 dream in which a choir of children, suspended in the air, sang in a strange language and presented harmonies and movements that Joseph worked into Ladysmith's act. The years that followed brought Joseph's revelation of Christian faith, many competition victories for Ladysmith, a recording career that has produced over 30 albums since 1970, collaboration with Paul Simon, and now, fame that rivals or tops that of any African performing group. After the murder of brother **Headman Shabalala** by an off-duty South African policeman in 1991, Joseph added his three sons into the lineup. Ladysmith's 1987 album, *Shaka Zulu*, successfully blends English and Zulu lyrics and remains the best introduction to their work.

◉ *Classic Tracks* (*Shanachie, US*) • **Shaka Zulu** (*Warner Bros., US*) • *Liph' Iqiniso* (*Shanachie, US*)
◉ *Various Artists,* **Mbube Roots** (*Rounder, US*)

JOHNNY CLEGG

When **Johnny Clegg** first brought his half-Zulu, half-white band **Juluka** to Europe, amazed audiences saw a young white man singing in Zulu, playing traditional guitar riffs and nailing difficult, high-kicking *indlamu* war dances with his lithe partner **Dudu Zulu**. French fans dubbed Johnny "Le Zoulou Blanc" (The White Zulu). Born in England, raised in Zimbabwe and Zambia, Johnny landed in Johannesburg, South Africa a shy, inarticulate boy of 12, who by his own account hated school and music. A chance encounter with an old Zulu street guitarist caught Johnny's ear, and led him to Zulu culture. Johnny teamed up with guitarist and songwriter **Sipho Mchunu** to form Juluka. In South Africa, Juluka alarmed authorities by presenting black and white musicians together on stage. When the group's potent marriage of Zulu war songs and English folk-rock caught on, Juluka faced bomb threats, concert shutdowns and racism from both the black and white music industries. Sipho retired to his farm in 1986, and Johnny formed a more western pop-oriented outfit called **Savuka**, which continues to record hits and wow audiences, especially abroad. Savuka performed its resonant tribute to political victims of apartheid, "Asimbonanga," at Nelson Mandela's inauguration. In the wake of Dudu Zulu's murder in 1993, and South Africa's new political reality, Johnny has moved on to new projects—a Juluka revival record, his first Sotho record, a new group, and a campaign to bolster South African pop on local radio and stages in the face of new international competition introduced by the lifting of apartheid's barriers.

◉ *Juluka,* **The Best of Juluka** (*Rhythm Safari, US*) • **Ubhule Bemvelo** (*Rhythm Safari, US*) • **Musa Ukungilandela** (*Rhythm Safari, US*) • **Universal Men** (*Rhythm Safari, US*) • **African Litany** (*Rhythm Safari, US*)
◉ *Savuka,* **In My African Dream: The Best of...** (*Rhythm Safari, US*) • **Shadow Man** (*Capitol, US*)

LUCKY DUBE

The shining star of African reggae, **Lucky Dube** made his first record in 1982, a Soul Brothers imitation produced by his cousin, singer **Richard Siluma**. Inspired by the public reaction to Jimmy Cliff's South African tours, Richard encouraged Lucky to try his hand at reggae. With his band the **Slaves**, Lucky then recorded *Rastas Never Die*, and by the late '80s, he had assumed the role of a message singer and earned a place along-side **Brenda Fassie**, **Stimela** and the **Soul Brothers** at the big outdoor music festivals that provided the only permitted venue for popular acts. Then in 1987, Lucky's album *Slave*, with its deeply resonant title song, sold 400,000 copies, to date the biggest selling album South Africa has seen. In its low register, Lucky's raspy voice invokes Peter Tosh, but Lucky can also unleash a smooth, powerful falsetto to rival Smokey Robinson. Lucky's tight grooves, passionate melodies and flutey keyboards have become a model for reggae bands throughout Africa. By 1991, Lucky had usurped Ivory Coast's **Alpha Blondy** as the top man in African reggae, and today he ranks as one of the top-selling artists on the continent. A sure sign of his credentials, Lucky has even won over the discerning crowd at Jamaica's annual Reggae Sunsplash festival. Recently, though, a large fraction of his band walked out on him taking up a new title, **Free at Last**.

⭕ *Slave* (Shanachie, US/Celluloid, France) • **House of Exile** (Shanachie, US) • **Victims** (Shanachie, US ⭕ **Free At Last**, (forthcoming) (Tusk, SA)

FOUR BROTHERS AND THE ZIMBABWE GUITAR SOUND

After Zimbabwe's independence, groups once resigned to copying British, American, Zairean and South African hits began to assert a strong local identity. A distinct guitar band sound developed, characterized by lively, independent guitar and bass lines—not unlike East African benga—and sweetly harmonized vocals that many compare to the early Beatles, as well as the thumping downbeat characteristic of much southern African music. **Jonah Moyo and Dvera Ngwena** along with **John Chibadura** emphasized the rumba side, while **James Chimombe** pressed the South African aspect. But one of the most versatile and per-sistent groups has proved to be the Shona quartet, the **Four Brothers**, headed by drummer and vocalist **Marshall Munhumumwe**, a nephew of Zimbabwe's pop legend **Thomas Mapfumo,** though the two are practically the same age. Marshall's group had split off from the **Great Sounds** in 1977, and when they went into the studio to record a song, they had no name. "Since you are four," said the producer, "I will write Four Brothers." From there, the hits began to flow, blending rumba, Shona tradition and the fast jit style in a small group format based around blistering guitar interaction. After playing the WOMAD festival in England in 1988, they returned with their own equipment and have cranked through the long nights in Harare's "dancing bars" ever since.

⭕ Four Brothers, **Makorokoto** (Cooking Vinyl, UK) • **Bros.**, (Cooking Vinyl, UK)
⭕ John Chibadura, **The Essential John Chibadura** (CSA, Germany) • **More of the Essential John Chibadura** (CSA, Germany)
⭕ Jonah Moyo & Devera Ngwena, **Taxi Driver** (K-KO) • **Follow the Crocodile** (One Heart)
⭕ Various, **Zimbabwe Frontline** (Stern's Earthworks) • **Spirit of the Eagle: Zimbabwe Frontline, v. 2** (Stern's Earthworks) • **Vibrant Zimbabwe** (ZimBob, US) • **Viva! Zimbabwe** (Hannibal, US & UK)

THOMAS MAPFUMO & THE BLACKS UNLIMITED

In the 1970s, Zimbabwe's *chimurenga* guerrillas fought a grizzly independence war against their white Rhodesian rulers. Reasserting African culture, revolution-era musicians from the Shona majority created a new pop sound based on the chiming, cyclic melodies and rhythms of the *mbira*, a kind of thumb piano used to contact ancestor spirits. A young rock-and-roll singer named **Thomas Mapfumo** popularized the *chimurenga* sound and still plays the music today with his band the **Blacks Unlimited**. Mapfumo means "spears" in Shona, and Thomas's early chimurenga singles, including "Mothers, Send Your Children to War" and "Trouble in the Communal Lands," lived up to his combative name. "People were being killed by soldiers," recalls Thomas. "They were running from their homes, and coming to live in town like squatters. Many used to cry when they listened to the lyrics of these songs." Provoked by his popularity, the authorities jailed Thomas briefly before the Rhodesian defeat in 1979.

Chimurenga transposed the complex, sinewy lines of mbira music onto guitars and bass, and put the triplet pattern played by the *hosho* shaker on the hi-hat, backed by a solid bass drum pulse. Thomas overlaid ethereal chants and deep-throated warbles, and peppered his arrangements with quirky horn section passages. In recent years, he has added as many as three mbiras to the lineup. Thomas still laces his songs with pointed messages, warning people not to abandon their ancestral ways, and attacking the devices of politicians, notably in his brave 1989 single, "Corruption." The '90s have seen renewed interest in traditional pop. Veteran mbira musicians like **Ephat Mujuru** and **Sekuru Gora** have recorded successful dance records, and a new generation of dance bands, including **Legal Lions, Sweet Melodies, Black Ites** and **Traditional Madness** have taken up the mbira pop sound.

⏺ **Chimurenga Singles** (*Shanachie, US*) • **Shumba:Vital Hits of Zimbabwe** (*Stern's Earthworks*) • **Ndangariro** (*Shanachie, US*) • **Corruption** (*Mango, US*) • **Chamunorwa** (*Mango, US*) • **Hondo** (*Zimbob, US*) **Vanhu Vatema** (*Zimbob, US*)

STELLA RAMBISAI CHIWESHE

One of Zimbabwe's few female *mbira* (thumb piano) players, **Stella Rambisai Chiweshe** grew up in the forest region of Mhondoro. As a child, Stella says, "I was always making a rhythm—on the door, on a dish—I played it on everything. I also liked to sing very much, and *loud*." Fascinated by music, Stella began drumming at eight and first attended an mbira ceremony at the age of sixteen. At the time, local missionaries called mbira music "Satan's work." And even when Stella moved with her mother to a province where mbira players lived, musicians did not want to teach a young girl. Eventually, Stella received the blessing of a family ancestor spirit and began to play, despite being told that no man would marry an mbira player. In 1974, her first single "Kasahwa" did so well that Stella developed a bad case of stage fright. She refused to play mbira on stage until 1984, when her musical career began in earnest. Today, Stella records both traditional and pop records. She works between homes in Germany and Zimbabawe. Her late '80s record *Ambuya?*, a collaboration with British musicians, presents a spirited mbira pop sound quite different from the one Thomas Mapfumo and his followers have developed in Zimbabwe.

⏺ **Ambuya?** (*GlobeStyle, UK*) • **Chisi** (*Piranha, Germany*) • **Kumusha** (*Piranha, Germany*) • **Shungu** (*Piranha, Germany*)

OLIVER MUTUKUDZI

With his soul-inflected *tuku* style, singer/songwriter/guitarist **Oliver Mutukudzi** alone rivals Thomas Mapfumo for the mantle of Zimbabwe pop's spiritual father. Born in 1952, Oliver recorded his first hits in the late '70s and remains active today. Though it occasionally nods to Shona traditional music, Oliver's sound typically lies somewhere between South African jive pop and classic r&b. Oliver adores Otis Redding above all, but his own husky, mellifluous voice sounds closer to Jamaica's Toots Hibbert. Claiming no overriding stylistic model, Oliver believes in the interrelatedness of all African music "from Cape Town to Cairo." Just the same Oliver's winning personality pervades his sound, rendering the tuku style instantly recognizable. Oliver always packs in a dance crowd at his frequent shows in Harare's active hotel/club scene. His rollicking songs and long-legged moves go down well, but Oliver says it's the message, not the beat, that sells his songs. Acting as a kind of national conscience, Oliver concentrates on family stories, sensitively exploring the social issues people face in their daily lives. Oliver's 1992

CD *Shoko* presents a set of classic tuku hits, crisply rerecorded in a German studio. For his part though, Oliver says he misses the "rawness" of the older productions. "They were more African than this digital thing coming up. We seem to be running away from something." Self-effacing and down-to-earth, Oliver runs a grocery store in his hometown when he's not working with his band.

⬤ **Shoko** (*Piranha, Germany*) • **Ziwere Mukopenhavn** (*Shava/Stern's*)
⬤ *Various,* **Jit—The Movie** (*Stern's Earthworks*)

BHUNDU BOYS

Few Afropop bands have risen as fast and fallen as tragically as Zimbabwe's **Bhundu Boys**. While other Harare groups struggled to meld borrowed and indigenous musical elements, this young quintet seemed to nail it from the moment they started in the heady days after the country's 1980 independence. Their early records, *Shabini* and *Tsvimbodzemoto*, crystallized the breakneck jit sound, but also showed that the group could condense a nine-minute Zairean rumba/soukous extravaganza into just three, and slam out jive to rival Soweto's finest. Tight players, sweet singers and natural composers, the Bhundus captured the freshness of the new Zimbabwe, and frontman **Biggie Tembo** and lead guitarist **Rise Kagona** delivered irresistable live energy and charisma. Within a few years, the band moved to Scotland, where they worked clubs throughout the U.K. and effectively broke the new Zimbabwe sound internationally. Their subsequent records awkwardly incorporated English lyrics and lacked the freshness of their first work, but the group's live energy sustained them. After touring Europe and

America repeatedly though, the Bhundus suffered the bitter defection of front man Biggie Tembo in 1990. The next year, bassist **David Mankaba** died after publicly announcing he suffered from AIDS. The remaining Bhundus recorded two more records. But after keyboard man and composer **Shakie Kangwena** also died in 1994, this pioneering band seems to have reached the end of its long, wild road.

⬤ **Shabini** (*Discafrique, UK*) • **Tsvimbodzimoto** (*Discafrique, UK*) • **Pamberi** (*Mango, US*) • **Live at King Tut's Wah Wah Hut** (*Cooking Vinyl, UK*)

LEONARD DEMBO

Back in Harare, the public continues to hunger for new local stars. So despite economic hardship, drought, scarcity of instruments and equipment and continued competition from Zairean and South African stars, new talent emerges year after year. Zimbabwe rumba acts like **Penga Udzoke**, the **Maugwe Brothers** and **Ketai & the Simba Brothers** draw the big dance crowds. But the biggest new name to emerge in the '90s is **Leonard Dembo** and his band the **Barura Express**. Slight and unassuming, Leonard touches audiences with his high, clear voice and lyrics in the Oliver Mutukudzi tradition, celebrating daily life. Leonard became a full-time musician in 1985. The name he chose for his group, Barura, means non-stop, and the group's trajectory lived up to the idea. Leonard built his audience steadily, but his big breakthrough came with his 1992

hit "Chitekete." Written years earlier during a break from his cattle herding chores, the songs paraphrases rural Shona sayings. It became so popular that for a while, it seemed every bride requested that it be played at her wedding. Sticking with the spare, guitar band sound, Leonard has a clear hit-making knack. "If a sound comes into my head three times," he says, "then I know it's a record."

⊙ **Chitekete** (Gramma, Zimbabwe)
Note: look for other releases on Gramma. Nothing is available internationally yet.

BLACK UMFOLOSI

scene, but few Ndebele pop bands join him there. Meanwhile, on the traditional front, Ndebele a capella group **Black Umfolosi** have built a reputation locally and even toured in Europe, Australia and America. Riding the success of South African *mbube* kings **Ladysmith Black Mambazo**, Black Umfolosi deliver their own brand of men's choral music. They sing the elegant religious and love songs Ladysmith popularized, but they also include a variety of traditional dances, including Zulu war dances complete with colorful shields and precise, dramatic foot-stomping and the somewhat lighter *gumboots dance*, in which dancers slap the tops of their tall rubber boots in complex, lock-step rhythms. Developed in the miners' hostels of South Africa and southern Zimbabwe, the gumboots dance presents an exciting and poignant expression of traditional culture in the colonial context.

Black Umfolosi performing traditional Zulu dances (left) and men's choral music (above).

⊙ **Unity** (World Circuit, UK)

While Shona groups dominate Zimbabwe's pop scene, the city of Bulawayo hosts musicians from the country's other major ethnic group, the Ndebele. Back in the '50s, Bulawayo guitarists **George Sibanda** and **Josaya Hadebe** developed highly influential, fingerpicking gui-

tar sounds heard through much of East and southern Africa. But since independence the Ndebele, closely related to the Zulu of South Africa, have had to struggle for musical recognition in Zimbabwe. **Lovemore Majaivana**, with his garish stage outfits and pumping jive rhythms, remains a fixture on the national

DAMA MAHALEO AND D'GARY

In the early '70s, the Indian Ocean island of Madagascar saw a period of fervent student unrest culminating in a socialist revolution in 1972. During the buildup to that watershed event, a teenage poet and singer, who admired Jacques Brel and Pete Seeger, electrified political rallies singing complex, heartfelt songs in Malagasy. From those promising beginnings, **Dama Mahaleo** created the most widely loved national group of the '70s, **Mahaleo**. Dama's lustrous tenor conveyed palpable passion in his songs of love and a changing society, and roots flavorings in the band's gentle pop appealed to a nation barely a decade into its independence. Mahaleo's popularity survived the dictatorship that grew from the '72 revolution, the rise of *salegy*, and the collapse of Madagascar's recording industry in the '80s. In 1992, Dama's ongoing quest for talented musicians from the rural areas led

him to **Ernest Randrianasolo** (a.k.a. **D'Gary**), a phenomenal guitar innovator. In the remote Bara village of Betroka, D'Gary grew up playing ukulele-like *kabosy*, the mouth bow and any other instrument he got his hands on. Using a borrowed guitar, D'Gary came up with 11 guitar tunings and a variety of fingerpicking techniques to convey the music of traditional instruments like the *valiha* and *marovany* harps and the kabosy. D'Gary's instrumental brilliance and sweet songs about nature and daily life proved a winning complement to Dama's artistry, and the next year, they recorded *The Long Way Home*, an adventurous duo album featuring guest spots by prominent musicians from Louisiana, where they recorded.

⊙ Dama and D'Gary, **The Long Way Home** (Shanachie, US)
⊙ D'Gary, **Malagasy Guitar** (Shanachie, US)

⊙ *D'Gary & Jihé,* **Horombe** *(Stern's Africa)*
⊙ *Dama,* **Melodies from Madagascar** *(Playasound, France)*
⊙ *Compilations that include Dama, D'Gary, Sammy, Rossy, others:* **Music from Madagascar** *(Buda, France)* • **Madagasikara 2: Current Popular Music of Madagascar** *(GlobeStyle, UK)* • *A World Out of Time: Henry Kaiser & David Lindley in Madagascar* *(Shanachie, US)* • **Madagaskari 1** *(Feuer und Eis, Germany)*

ROSSY

Paul Bert Rahasimanana (a.k.a. **Rossy**) grew up surrounded by music in a poor neighborhood in Antananarivo,

Madagascar. He began to play at the age of seven when a friend gave him an accordion, an instrument inexplicably common in Madagascar. With no instruction, Rossy began learning songs off the radio and soon formed a band with some high school friends. After school, Rossy went to live for a while with his estranged father in the northeast coastal region, home of the popular, galloping electric pop music known as *salegy*. Though the '70s produced many salegy singles and tapes on the DiscoMad label, the bands never played in the highland capital Antananarivo. "It's a shock when you come from the highlands," says Rossy, recalling the wild atmosphere and sexual openness he found up north. "Every Saturday, there was a ball with dancing. All the masters of salegy were there—**Roger Georges** and **Tianjamani**—the top groups in Madagascar." When Rossy got back to his band, he proved himself a musical omnivore, taking up guitar, the *valiha* harp, traditional flute and singing in every style he heard. Probably the most popular act in the country, the **Rossy Band** combine the gentle traditions of the highlands, the rambunctious triplet rhythms of salegy, and later rock, reggae and South African pop styles. By the mid-'80s, Rossy owned instruments for his band, a sound system, and a bus which he still uses to travel all over Madagascar playing shows for a loyal national audience. In 1993, Rossy recorded his signature international release, *One Eye on the Future, One Eye on the Past*.

⊙ **One Eye on the Future, One Eye on the Past** *(Shanachie, US)* • **Island of Ghosts** *(RealWorld, UK)*

TARIKA SAMMY AND TARIKA

Tarika Sammy—"Sammy's Group"—began as a traditional, all-occasions outfit consisting of multi-instrumentalist **Sameola Andriamalalaharijaona,** known simply as Sammy, and whatever musicians he chose to play with for the occasion. Despite his remarkable and diverse talents, Sammy concluded in 1991 that a musician couldn't earn a decent living playing roots music. He considered getting a synthesizer and going electric, but singing sisters **Hanitra** (pictured at right) and **Noro Rasoanaivo** persuaded him to revamp Tarika Sammy once again. The new group's musicality and showmanship and their broad range of Malagasy folk styles brought them success previously reserved only for electric pop bands. Tarika Sammy toured internationally and recorded a landmark debut album, *Fanafody,* which helped inspire an enthusiastic audience for Malagasy music in Europe and the US. Sammy and his brother sang cool harmonies and played rippling cascades of melody on exotic instruments—the double-sided *jejy voatavo* harp with its calabash resonator; the elegant *marovany,* a box zither; the *valiha,* a bamboo tube with bicycle brake cable strings that produces a delicate, harp-like sound; and the *kabosy,* which jangles like a dulcimer when strummed in the quick polyrhythms that animate Malagasy music. Hanitra sang bright harmonies and danced with her sister, and also charmed international audiences with frank descriptions of Malagasy musical occasions—weddings, circumcisions and the celebratory exhumation of ancestors' bones. Sammy and his brother went their own way in 1993, and Hanitra and Noro recruited three talented instrumentalists to replace them in a new group simply called **Tarika.**

◉ *Tarika Sammy,* **Fanafody** (Rogue, UK/Green Linnet, US) • **Balance** (Rogue, UK/Xenophile, US)
◉ *Tarika,* **Bibiango** (Rogue, UK/Xenophile, US)

Above: Hanitra of Tarika

NEW STARS OF MADAGASCAR

Though international audiences have mostly heard the roots pop and traditional folk music of Madagascar, present day groups adapt hard rock, Zairean soukous, bubblegum pop and a variety of other foreign sounds flooding local airwaves. Schooled in the Paris soukous scene after his years playing with Zairean guitarist **Diblo Dibala,** guitarist/singer **Freddy de Majunga** has pioneered *salegy-rumba.* Salegy stalwarts like **Jaojoby Eusebe** and **Jean-Fredy** remain popular, despite the rise of a promising crop of younger salegy stars, including singer **Mily Clément** and groups **Zaza Club** and **Ejema.** Charting a new course, singer **Feon'ala** mixes pop elements in search of a new fusion sensation. Meanwhile, another powerful vocalist **Randimbiarison** (known as **Ricky**) has inspired a phenomenon dubbed "Rickymania" in the local press. Ricky's crack band includes bassist **Toty,** whose playing evokes the deep, droning resonance of the traditional marovany box zither. Ricky's update of the old *vako-drazana* folk tradition, which he calls *vakojazzana,* has inspired one seasoned observer of the Madagascar scene to select him as the likely Malagasy superstar of the '90s. Meanwhile, the **Justin Vali Trio,** based in Paris, forges an international roots sound that took them all the way to Woodstock '94.

◉ *Various,* **World Beat, Vol. 7—Madagascar** (Celluloid, France)
◉ *Justin Vali,* **Rambala** (Silex, France)
◉ *The Justin Vali Trio,* **The Truth/(My Marina)** (RealWorld, UK)
◉ *Tsinjaka,* **Tsinjaka** (Rogue, UK)
◉ *Jaojoby Eusebe,* **Jaojoby: Salegy!** (Rogue, UK)
◉ *Mily Clément,* **Banja Malalaka** (Playasound, France)
◉ *Mama Sana,* **The Legendary Mama Sana** (Shanachie, US)

ZAMBIA

Tucked between Zaire, Zimbabwe and Angola, landlocked Zambia has only recently sprouted the beginnings of a music industry capable of delivering the country's distinctive, highly localized pop to a wider audience. After the discovery of copper in the 1920s, mining communities in the north supported itinerant, guitar-toting troubadours like **Stephen Tsotsi Kasumali** and **Isaac Matafwani.** Their music drew from the same cultural well as did the Shaba region guitar pickers of southern Zaire, important progenitors of later Congolese styles. The '70s and early '80s saw the development of electric pop bands in the Zambian capital Lusaka, but despite President Kenneth Kaunda's attempts to suppress foreign sounds, pan-African music from Kenya, Tanzania, Angola and South Africa still dominated the commercial mix, mostly excluding input from Zambia's own 73 ethnic groups. In the past decade, though, bands like the multi-ethnic **Amayenge** and the farmer brothers of **Shalawambe**—which means "keep on gossiping"—have pressed the development of homegrown Zambian pop. The result, dubbed *kalindula* after a one-string, barrel bass from Luapula province, has a gritty appeal that caught on nicely once recorded and distributed in the '80s. Kalindula has become an umbrella term for a growing range of Zambian pop, but the original sound features rolling triplet rhythms, guitar work that slides between rumba stylings, local melodies transferred from traditional instruments, and tricky copperbelt region fingerpicking topped off with down-home, call-and-response vocals, often between a lead singer and a harmonized chorus. Live music ebbs and flows in Lusaka these days, but a new wave of kalindula groups, including **Mashabe, Bwaluka Founders** and the **Junior Mulemena Boys,** now give pervasive Zairean hits a run for their money in the country's popular beerhalls.

◉ *Alick Nkhata,* **Shalapo** (RetroAfric, UK)
◉ *Various,* **Zambiance** (GlobeStyle, UK) • **Shani, The Sounds of Zambia** (WOMAD) • *Various,* **From the Copperbelt... Zambian Miners' Songs** • *Various,* **Guitar Songs from Tanzania, Zambia and Zaire** (Original Music, US)
◉ *Amayenge,* **Ameyenge** (Mondeca/Demon)
◉ *Shalawambe,* **Samora Machel** (Mondeca/Demon)

ANGOLA

Born in 1942 in Portuguese-ruled Angola, **Barceló De Carvalho**, a.k.a. **Bonga Kuenda,** grew up to become a much loved professional soccer player. But when he turned to singing pro-independence songs, the country's right wing regime forced him into exile. Even after Angola won its independence in 1975, Bonga stayed in Paris and Lisbon, connecting with musicians from other Portuguese-speaking countries—Brazil, Mozambique, Cape Verde and Guinea Bissau, and recording Afropop albums. Angola's most visible pop artist, Bonga sings in a gruff, melancholy growl reminiscent of an old Brazilian *sambista*. Saddened by his country's long civil war, Bonga says he pressed on with his music in order to give people something beautiful and human with which to balance images of strife. Angola's recording industry, which once turned out singles and LPs of *semba*—ancestor of the Brazilian samba— *merengue*, *pachanga* and other styles, declined during the war, but even then, live bands

continued to play in public halls. True survivors, **Orquestra Os Jovens Do Prenda**, started out as a rural marimba, percussion and vocal group in 1965. Adding three electric guitars, bass, horns and trap drums to their five-piece percussion section, the band made the transition to the capital, Luanda, during the 1970s. The early years of the civil war forced them to split up, but they reformed in 1981. Os Jovens Do Prenda blend the indigenous semba rhythm with Zairean rumba and

a style they call *quilapanga*—Angolan merengue. Berlin Festa!, a rare live recording the band made in 1990, offers one of the only available examples of homegrown Angolan pop. Other top names in Angolan pop include **Eduardo Paim**, **Paulo Flores**, **Valdamar Bastos**, and **Ruka Vandunen**.

Left: Bonga Kuenda

⚫ Bonga, **Paz em Angola** (Rounder, US) • **Angola** (Playasound, France)
⚫ Eduardo Paim, **Mae Africa** (EMI) • **Foi Aqui** (Lusafrica, France)
⚫ Kafala Brothers, **Ngola** (Stern's, UK)
⚫ Waldemar Bastos, **Pitanga Madura** (Valentim de Carvalho/EMI, Portugal)
⚫ Orqestra Os Jovens Do Prenda, **Orqestra Os Jovens Do Prenda: Berlin Festa!** (Piranha, Germany)
⚫ Trio AKA, **Mama Christina** (Stern's, UK)

MOZAMBIQUE

Civil war followed close on the heels of the end of Portuguese rule in Mozambique, as in Angola. But even while the South African-controlled RENAMO guerrillas terrorized the population during the late '70s and '80s, the country's most popular band **Marabenta Star** broadcast from the national radio station. *Marabenta* describes

an urban party where musicians try out their stuff, and it's also a hopped-up version of the local *majika* rhythm. In Marabenta Star's musical stew, guitars mix rock and *soukous* licks, horns add spicy Latin bravado, and a big, percussion-rich rhythm section stirs up grooves dense with local and foreign ingredients. Front and center, velvety, horn-like voices

sing tales of everyday life in African languages, something that irked the Portuguese authorities in the band's early days. The group **Ghorwane** also plays a Mozambican take on big band Afropop. Led by **Tchika Fernando** and named for a lake that provides scarce water in the dry Gaza region, this group uses horns, guitars, percussion and strong vocal harmonies to adapt local rhythms—*xigubu*, *mapiko*, *tufu* and *marabenta*. **Zena Baker** and **Abdul Remane Gion**'s band **Eyuphuru** comes from an island in the northeast and favors a folky, acoustic guitar-based sound, with some influence from the nearby Swahili culture. Zena's cool, at times jazzy vocals, and the group's sophisticated acoustic/electric arrangements set them apart from both traditional groups and from dance bands like Marabenta Star and Ghorwane. Mozambique's war years ended with the election of 1994, hopefully opening the door for more of its great musicians to develop careers.

Left: Ghorwane

⚫ Orquestra Marrabenta Star de Moçambique, **Independence** (Piranha, Germany) • **Piquenique** (Piranha, Germany)
⚫ Ghorwane, **Majurugenta** (RealWorld, UK)
⚫ Eyuphoro, **Mama Mosambiki** (RealWorld, UK)
⚫ Eduardo Durao, **Timbila** (GlobeStyle, UK)
⚫ Various, **!Saba Saba!** (GlobeStyle, UK) • **Music From Mozambique, v. 1-2** (GobeStyle, UK) • **Mozambique One, Mozambique Two** (GlobeStyle, UK)

CENTRAL AND EAST AFRICA

Modern African traditions represent the successive layering of cultural ideas over time. The things that survive today reflect unknowable African pre-history, colonial-era oddities, and of course, the scrambled bric-a-brac of our high-tech media age. The music from present day countries Zaire and Congo—variously called *Congo music, Zairois, rumba* and now *soukous*—presents a compelling example. Early in the century, townsfolk along the Congo River relaxed by dancing to *maringa*—thumb-piano, drum, and bottle percussion music, drawn from various ethnic groups: Kongo, Lulua, Luba and others newly united by the emerging trade language, Lingala. When West Indian immigrants and sailors with guitars arrived in port cities, and later, when Cuban pop recordings flooded radio airwaves, Central Africans naturally found themselves in the music that Caribbean descendants of Congolese slaves had helped to create, and they reappropriated it.

In Zairean pop records from the '50s, you hear the click pattern of the Afro-Cuban *clave*, and singers adapting the nasal quality of Havana's *rumberos*. But the African Lingala melodies possess a unique cadence and flow that define a timeless vocal sound. And guitars spin mesmerizing cycles that suggest a fresh infusion of African roots. Early Kinshasa bands like Joseph Kabasele's **African Jazz** and **Franco's OK Jazz** played *cha-chas, biguines, boleros* and *rumbas*. The sound they settled on was in fact closest to Cuban *son*, but they called it rumba and the name stuck.

Rumba cut across ethnic, linguistic, national and generational barriers, quickly spilling over into East Africa, where Luo, Kikuyu and other peoples adapted the guitar-based sound to the twists and turns of their own local rhythms, melodies and languages. Once again, fresh styles with deep and deepening histories came to life adding new hues and patterns to Afropop's emerging mosaic.

The central swath of Africa—from French colonial Brazzaville and Belgian-built Kinshasa in the west, to the Muslim spice island of Zanzibar in the east—contains a daunting array of peoples and cultures. Frenzied, neo-traditional pop from the Baluba of the Kasai regions at the center of the continent could not be more different from the serene, Arab- and Asian-tinged taarab ensembles and orchestras of Kenya's port city, Mombasa. But the Congo's rumba sound has touched all the people of this region, and beyond, so this section begins with and concentrates on that story.

Things have changed for the worse in Zaire since the destructive, failed army rebellion of 1991, but when we visited Kinshasa in the mid- and late-'80s, the music quarter of Matonge bustled 24-hours-a-day, fueled on local music. Record stores pointed speakers onto the hot, dusty streets and blared the latest hits by **Zaiko Langa Langa**, **Mbilia Bel** and **Franco**. Families at roadside stalls hawked coffee, cigarettes, and boiled eggs with hot pepper alongside household supplies like

Above: Papa Wemba on Kinshasa billboard   Top: Kinshasa attractions

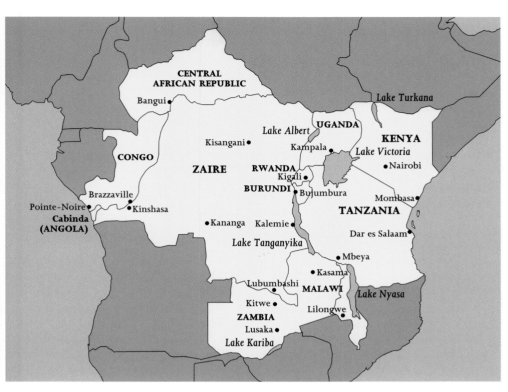

ruption, desperate economic failure, and the attempted military uprising of 1991, he has held on ever since. Mobutu instilled a deep fear of dissent and sadly failed to develop his country's vast resources. But the walls he built around his people and his attempts to boost cultural and national pride certainly contributed to the environment that bred Africa's most influential pop music.

Kenya and Tanzania, the East African nations discussed in this section, have enjoyed more varied political fortunes since independence. In Kenya, following the brutal British suppression of the Mau Mau uprising in the mid-'50s, Jomo Kenyatta took power and ran a tight, pro-western, but decidedly non-democratic one-party state until his death in 1978. His successor, the current president Daniel Arap Moi, has spoken of turning the country into a non-ethnic, open democracy, but so far hasn't lived up to his rhetoric. First a German and then a British colony, Tanzania came together under the idealistic, socialist leadership of Julius Nyerere from 1961-85. Though he worked to counter the ethnicity-based politics that plagued other new Africa nations, and received help from a number of countries, Nyerere's economic policies bred poverty and debt. Today, Zanzibar and the rest of Tanzania live under separate governments, moving slowly, but peacefully toward becoming more democratic societies.

soap and toilet paper. On the weekends, they'd sell all night, confident that people moving from one open air club or smoky bar to another might need something along the way. Wealthier folks from other neighborhoods poured into Matonge for its dusk-to-dawn nightlife. Early in the evening, nameless groups, sometimes still in their teens, took up the house-owned instruments to deliver a few original songs and show off their own synchronized dance moves. Once the club's headline act—maybe **Choc Stars** or romantic singer **Koffi Olomide**—took the stage, couples sipping tall bottles of beer would casually make their way to the dance floor, to move close with cool understatement. Only in the fast, reveling *seben* passages, where singers would entice the crowd to follow their latest moves, would couples break apart and shake, before returning to sip their beers. Though the music lasted until first light, few seemed to get drunk, and the dancers maintained impeccable control.

Zairean music adheres rigorously to rules and decorum, affecting the roles of the instruments, the progression of rhythms in a song, and precision matching of voice quality and rhythms in the vocal harmonies. The music's feeling of unbridled joy begins with discipline. This unusual rigor mirrors aspects of the strict social and political climate that has nurtured the Zaire sound.

Late in the last century, Belgium's King Léopold established a particularly cruel colonial government in the Belgian Congo, which lasted until 1959 when violence forced the

Belgians to relinquish power. Patrice Lumumba became prime minister, only to be murdered in a coup a few months later. General anarchy and inter-ethnic warfare followed, sending many refugees, including rumba musicians, into Uganda, Kenya and Tanzania, among other places. Then in 1965, Mobutu Sese Seko took over, and despite massive cor-

Old town and harbor, Mombasa

RUMBA PIONEERS

Joseph Kabasele (a.k.a. **Le Grand Kalle**) and his band **African Jazz** heralded Zaire's independence in 1960 with the song "Independence Cha Cha." Kalle had a

sweet, pure solo voice that inspired many imitators. But major credit for the band's massive popularity also goes to guitarist **Nicolas "Dr Nico" Kasanda**, a descendent of the Luba people of central Zaire like many of Congolese music's great contributors. A mere boy in when he started in 1957, Nico rose to stardom playing with Kalle, and then formed his own band **African Fiesta** after splitting off from Kalle in the early '60s. Nico had a lyrical touch on guitar, playing circular patterns during singing passages, and soloing with sensual eloquence. Today's best-known *soukous* guitarist, **Diblo Dibala** calls Nico "the school of Zairean guitar." Nico's late '60s work also displays heartthrob performances by vocalist **Sangana**. As other bands rose during the '60s and '70s, Nico fell into obscurity. He made his final recordings in Togo, not long before he died in a Brussels hospital in 1985.

In a competitive and highly fluid environment where bands formed and dispersed constantly, **Franco** (a.k.a. **Luambo Makiadi**) kept his group **OK Jazz** together for 33 years. It grew from the tidy six-piece outfit to the 20- or 30-piece megaband that survived him

when he died at age 51 in 1989. Given his extensive legacy of recordings, and the host of careers he launched and nurtured, Franco can justly be called the Duke Ellington of Zairean music. "On Entre OK, On Sort KO" (one enters OK, one leaves KO'd) was the band's early motto. Later dubbed **TPOK Jazz**—adding TP for tout puissant or "all powerful"—the band played the Cuban sounds, but Franco also made prominent use of rhythms and themes from the village. His guitar playing—raw, aggressive and loaded with rhythmic subtleties—earned him the title "Sorcerer of the Guitar." And his musical arrangements grew to include batteries of guitars, horns and vocalists layering musical conversations over drums, bass and percussion. A chronicler of the turbulent nation-building he lived through, Franco's commentaries on social issues, sexual relations, tribalism, sorcery, and many other topics always struck a chord with the public, and with the fickle authorities, who awarded him the medal for the Order of the Leopard, only to take it away while jailing him for singing obscene lyrics a few years later.

Franco's biggest competition during the 1970s came from singer and composer **Tabu Ley Rochereau**, who left African Jazz to

become hugely popular singing with Dr. Nico's **African Fiesta**. After recording many classic songs, Rochereau formed his own band **Afrisa International,** which went on to blaze the trail for the European soukous invasion. Tabu Ley, the first Zairean bandleader to use trap drums in his sound, worked to internationalize the music. In 1971, Tabu Ley played a historic concert at Paris's Olympia theater, signaling the start of an exodus of Zairean musicians to the French capital. Less folkloric than OK Jazz, Afrisa went in for the big show with dancers, horn solos and arrangements that border on campy. At center stage, Tabu Ley spotlighted his own bell-like tenor voice. Using a succession of

Left: Tabu Ley Rochereau   Below: Franco

illustrious female vocalists, Tabu Ley spoke to all Africans by playing out lovers' dramas on stage, most notably with honey-toned chanteuse **Mbilia Bel**, who stirred a major scandal when she ended her collaboration and her romance with Tabu Ley to strike out on her own in Paris in 1988.

⬤ *Grand Kalle & African Jazz,* **Merveilles du Passé:V. 1-2** *(Sonodisc, France)*
⬤ *Various,* **Les Merveilles du Passé: 1957-75** *(Sonodisc, France)*
⬤ *Franco et al,* **Roots of OK Jazz, 1955-56** *(Crammed Discs, Belgium)*
⬤ *Franco and OK Jazz,* **Originalité** *(RetroAfric, UK)*
⬤ *Franco and TPOK Jazz,* **20 Anniversaire, v. 1-2** *(Sonodisc, France)*
⬤ *Franco and Sam Mangwana,* **Cooperation** *(Sonodisc, France)*
⬤ *Franco and TPOK Jazz,* **Mario** *(Sonodisc, France)* • **En Colere** *(Sonodisc, France)*
⬤ **Nico, Kwamy, Rochereau, Roger and African Fiesta,** *(Sonodisc, France)*
⬤ **Nico and African Fiesta Sukisa,** *1967-69, (Sonodisc, France)*
⬤ *Tabu Ley,* **Rochereau & L'Afrisa International, 1971-77** *(Sonodisc, France)* • **Babeti Soukous** *(RealWorld, UK)* • **Sarah** *(Genidia, France)* • **Man From Kinshasa** *(Shanachie, US)* • **En Amour y a pas de Calcul** *(Genidia,*

France)* • **Muzina** *(Rounder, US)* • **Exil Ley** *(Tamaris/Sonodisc, France)*
⬤ *Mbilia Bel,* **Keyna and Cadence Mudanda** *(Genidia/Sonodisc, France)* • **Phenomene** *(Mélodie, France)* • **Eswi Yo Wapi** *(FDB, France)*

⬤ *Doctor Nico,* **Doctor Nico** *(Original Music, US)*

Above: Mbilia Bel

Below left: Zaiko Langa Langa   Below: Pepe Kalle

THE ZAIKO GENERATION

With the worldwide spread of rock-and-roll in the late '60s, younger Zairean musicians looked for ways to strip rumba music down and rev it into a higher gear. Leading the way, a band of relatively well-to-do students calling themselves **Zaiko Langa Langa** came together in 1969 and turned the scene upside down. The name derived from a phrase that means "Zaire of our ancestors," a concept that dovetailed nicely with Zairean President Mobutu Sese Seko's *authenticité* policy of the early '70s. To Zaiko's good fortune, authenticity encouraged modern expressions of ancestral tradition to balance what Mobutu portrayed as the corrupting legacy of colonialism.

Zaiko revolutionized the older rumba music by dropping the horn section and focusing the attention on high-energy, three-guitar workouts, percussion and shouting chants known as *animation*. A common animation, "Pésa! Pésa!," means essentially "Give it up!" Zaiko gave the music a rock-and-roll edge and unprecedented youth appeal, conveying its natural romanticism into sweaty high gear. Zaiko songs start by telling an amorous story in the old rumba style and then lift into a

mid-tempo section with beautifully arranged call-and-response vocals before hitting the fast *seben* section.

Kinshasa's bustling club scene had no peer in Africa during the 1970s and '80s. In the music quarter called Matonge, clubs stayed open until sunrise, jamming to the seben sound that audiences demanded. In Zaiko's over-the-top seben formulation, the snare drum crashes out folkloric rhythms, the guitars weave and soar into the high frets, the singers shout out staccato, free-form animation and dance loose-hipped unison routines often for twenty minutes at a stretch. As the Kinshasa scene heated up in the 1970s, popular dances developed. Zaiko would lead the audience through playful moves, creating new crazes regularly, and giving them names like *zekete-zekete*, *volant* ("*driver*"), *sonzo-ma*, *cavacha* and *kwassa-kwassa*.

Establishing the pattern for Zairean bands to come, Zaiko underwent many battles of ego within the front-line and continually spawned offshoot groups—**Grand Zaiko Wawa, Langa Langa Stars, Viva la Musica,** and ultimately, two bands using the name Zaiko Langa Langa. By 1980, Zaiko was no longer just a group, but a whole clan of bands, a musical movement with more and more social trappings. Founding Zaiko vocalist **Papa Wemba** gets credit for launching the clan's trademark use of high fashion as a form of social rebellion. Wemba's dashing self-styled look—a 1930s throwback featuring baggy,

pleated trousers hemmed above shiny brogues and hair clipped close at the sides—soon earned him the title Pope of the *Sapeurs*: Society of Ambianceurs and Persons of Elegance. The Sapeurs elevate a clothing fetish to a spiritual level to the extent of boasting their own "religion" called *Katinda*, which means cloth. The wildness of soukous and the excesses of

the Sapeurs can be seen as channeled expressions of free spirits in an environment of political oppression and relentless conformity. During three decades of iron-fisted rule, Mobutu stifled all criticism of his government, and even enforced a national dress code for bureaucrats and businessmen.

Other greats of the Zaiko generation include female singers **M'Pongo Love** and **Tshala Muana**—queen of the rootsy mutuashi style. A long list of popular bands includes **Choc Stars** and their split-off rivals **Anti-Choc**— as in an electric shock—as well as **Bella Bella, Victoria Eleison** and **Empire Bakuba** fronted by the sweet-voiced **Pepe Kalle**, who at 300-plus pounds, rivaled Franco's girthy majesty on stage. The success of mutuashi, which avoids rumba and explores the 6/8 rhythms of central Zaire's Luba people, has led to other non-soukous developments. The rowdy urban folklore of **Swede Swede** uses mostly percussion, and also substitutes harmonica and accordion for soukous's guitars. These days though **Wenge Musica,** a student band much in the Zaiko Langa Langa mold, tops the Kinshasa scene.

◐ Zaiko Langa Langa, **Zaire-Ghana** (RetroAfric, UK) • **L'Authentique Zaiko Langa Langa** (Sonodisc, France) • **Nippon Banzai** (Sonodisc, France) • **Jetez L'Éponge** (Careere, France)
◐ Papa Wemba & Viva La Musica, **Love Kilawu** (Sonodisc, France) • **Foridoles** (Sonodisc, France)
◐ Papa Wemba, **Papa Wemba** (Celulloid, France/Stern's, UK) • **Emotion** (RealWorld, UK)

○ Pepe Kalle, **Gigantafrique!**, (GlobeStyle, UK) • **L'Argent Ne Fait Pas Le Bonheur** (Gefraco, France/Stern's Africa, UK)
○ Pepe Kalle & Nyboma, **Moyibe** (Syllart/Stern's, UK)
○ Choc Stars, **Engombe** (FDB, France)
○ Bozi Boziana, Deyess and Anti-Choc, **La Sirène** (Bade Stars, France)
○ Orchestre Vévé, **The Best Collection** (Sonodisc, France)
○ Evoloko Joker, **Mingalina B-52** (FDB, France)
○ Victoria Eleison, **V. 1-3** (FDB, France)
○ Tshala Muana, **Biduaya** (Celluloid, France) • **Soukous Siren** (Shanachie, US)
○ Wenge Musica, **Bouger Bouger** (Africassette, US) • **Kin E Bouge** (Mabisa, France)
○ Swede Swede, **Toleki Bango** (Crammed Discs, Belgium)

Left: Tshala Muana Above: Papa Wemba, and his stylish dancers (below)

SOUKOUS AMBASSADORS

As the competitive music scene in Kinshasa swelled after 1960, singers and players moved on to become bigger fish in smaller ponds. Franco's protégé, lead guitarist **Mose Se "Fan Fan,"** left Kinshasa to work in Kenya and Tanzania before settling in London in the '80s with his band **Somo Somo**. In 1993, Fan Fan joined Brussels-based OK Jazz alumni to launch one of many post-Franco spin-off groups, **Bana OK**. An inveterate wanderer, "Le Pigeon Voyageur" **Sam Mangwana** started out in Kinshasa as one of the few singers to work with both Franco and Tabu Ley. Sam then moved to Abidjan in 1976 where he launched his widely acclaimed group the **African All Stars,** and embarked on a rambling international career that continues today.

In the 1980s, *soukous* took hold in Paris and other European culture centers. Many musicians relocated to record and build careers away from home. Some recorded for the Zaire market, but others abandoned the demands of a fussy Kinshasa public and set out in new directions. Composer **Ray Lema** ventured into arty rock formulations and world music collaborations with, among others, a female Bulgarian choir. Few talk about Ray back home anymore, but other musicians have walked a finer line, managing to branch out without losing their base audience. Paris-based **Papa Wemba** maintains two bands, **Viva la Musica** for soukous, and a group including French session players for his international pop.

Among the soukous loyalists, **Les Quatre Etoiles** (**Four Stars**) united veterans of the Kinshasa scene, guitarists **Syran M'Benza** and **Bopol**, and singers **Wuta Mayi** and **Nyboma**, whose creamy tenor shines, even from the ranks of Zairean vocalists. The first Paris supergroup, Les Quatre Etoiles played soukous preened and polished for a European audience, and they remain popular. Another Paris success story, singer **Kanda Bongo Man** created a new model for soukous. By eliminating the slow rumba section from the long Zaiko song form and going straight for the seben, Kanda pioneered short, dance tracks suitable for play on disco dance floors everywhere. Groups like **Loketo** and **Soukous Stars** followed suit. Soon Paris became home to a loose federation of talented studio players who recorded in ever-shifting configurations, supporting singers on records for the African and Caribbean markets and filling out bands for occasional tours.

The cherubic Kanda, a graduate of the smooth Kinshasa band **Bella Bella**, brought sunny showmanship and a high degree of professionalism to the music. At first, his neat sound held limited appeal in Kinshasa, but

as his hit-making credentials built steadily, he began touring Africa in the early '90s, becoming one of the top-selling artists across the continent and even earning approval in his old hometown. One of the newest groups to emerge from the Paris scene, the immensely popular **Nouvelle Generation** spun off from **Papa Wemba's Viva la Musica** in 1992.

Soukous guitarists can earn cult followings, and Kanda's first guitarist **Diblo Dibala** garnered one of the most fanatical. Having played briefly with OK Jazz and then with Bella Bella and other groups back home, Diblo came to Paris and rose with Kanda, gracing his records with quick, stylish and elegantly precise seben solos. Diblo went on to work with Pepe Kalle and others before joining affable Congolese vocalist **Aurlus Mabele** to form the group **Loketo** in 1986. Loketo's early US tours helped to introduce soukous in America. Diblo and Aurlus parted ways in 1991, but Loketo forges on with an aggressive tour schedule, as does Diblo's new group **Matchatcha,** named for a flower that makes you itch—"to dance" says Diblo. Other pillars of the Paris soukous guitar stable include **Nene Tchakou, Lokassa Ya Mbongo, Dally Kimoko** and **Bamundele Virigo (Rigo Star).**

Some lovers of the old Kinshasa sounds complain about the Paris soukous machine. They say that the well-oiled studio system lets producers crank out records programmed on auto pilot using a handful of session players. Seen as signs of modernity by many in Africa, the keyboards and drum machines so

Above: Les Quatre Etoiles   *Top right: Kanda Bongo Man*

prevalent in Paris soukous can turn off western listeners who are attracted to African pop for its human feel and intimacy. In general, though, the complaint makes little sense to Zairean pop musicians who partially base their continued popularity on staying abreast of new developments in pop sound technology.

Meanwhile, back in Kinshasa, elements in the Zairean army rebelled against President Mobutu in 1991 creating a political and economic crisis from which the country has yet to emerge. The clubs of Matonge, which had supported hundreds of bands, went into decline. Since that watershed year, Zairean musicians have continued to emigrate to East Africa and recently, South Africa as well, the one African country where soukous was not previously heard due to the cultural restrictions accompanying apartheid. Many Zairean musicians have also gone to London, Paris, Brussels and other European cities. With competition fierce in Europe, some find their way to the US. Tabu Ley relocated to California in 1994 for a two year stay, and soukous bands run by Zairean expatriates now carry on the tradition in San Diego, North Carolina, Boston and New York.

Left: Elektra and Diblo Dibala

⚫ *Mose Se Fan Fan,* **Belle Epoque** (RetroAfric, UK)
⚫ *Sam Mangwana,* **Aladji** (Shanachie, US) • **Rumba Music** (Stern's Africa)
⚫ *4 Stars,* **Sangonini** (Stern's Africa, UK) • **6 Tubes/6 Hits** (Syllart, France)
⚫ *Bopol,* **The Best of Bopol** (Mélodie, France)
⚫ *Syran M'Benza,* **Symbiose** (Stern's, UK)
⚫ *Nyboma,* **Doublé, Doublé** (Rounder, US)
⚫ *Kanda Bongo Man,* **Sai-Liza** (Mélodie, France) • **Zing Zong** (Hannibal/Rykodisc, US) • **Soukous in Central Park** (Hannibal/Rykodisc, US)
⚫ *Shimita & Soukous Stars,* **Shimita & Soukous Stars** (Mélodie, France)
⚫ *Lokassa & Soukous Stars,* **Gozando** (Mélodie, France/Stern's, UK)
⚫ *Loketo,* **Soukous Trouble** (Shanachie, US) • **Extra Ball** (Shanachie, US)
⚫ *Matchatcha,* **Best of Diblo Dibala & Matchatcha** (Afric Music, France)
⚫ *Nouvelle Generation,* **Porokondo** (Flash Diffusion Business, France)
⚫ *Bana OK,* **Bakitani** (Stern's)
⚫ *Various,* **Heartbeat Soukous** (Stern's Earthworks)
⚫ *Ray Lema,* **Medecine** (Celluloid, France) • **Gaia** (Celluloid, France)

BANTOUS DE LA CAPITAL

Across the Congo River—or Fleuve Zaire—from Kinshasa, lies the sister city of Brazzaville, capital of the ex-French colony, the Republic of Congo. While these neighboring countries have weathered warm and chilly official relations over the past 40 years, their capital cities have nurtured parallel strains of rumba. During the '50s, Congolese musicians like singer **Edo Ganga,** guitarist **Papa Noel,** clarinetist **Jean-Serge Essous** and saxophonist **Nino Malapet** helped launch rumba music in Kinshasa. Born in 1934, Essous in particular energized the original **OK Jazz** lineup in 1956. Having crossed the river with his own band **Negro Jazz** a few years earlier, Essous brought valuable professionalism to the young Franco's fledgling band. When the Republic of Congo won its independence from France in 1960, a surge of nationalism led many France-based Congo musicians, including key members of OK Jazz, to return and establish careers in their new country. Noel, Ganga, Malapet and Essous went home to form **Orchestre Bantous,** later renamed **Les Bantous de la Capitale.** Though politics mostly kept them apart, Les Bantous and OK Jazz stayed close in spirit and developed along similar lines. Although less innovative than the Kinshasa scene, Brazzaville held its own as rumba spread, particularly when Les Bantous introduced the *boucher* dance craze in 1965. Having led Les Bantous during the '80s, singer **Pamelo Mounka** now has an offshoot group called **Bantous Movement.** Les Bantous remain active under the leadership of Nino Malapet, hewing close to the big band rumba sound.

⚫ *Les Bantous,* **Merveilles du Passé, 1963-1969** (Sonodisc, France) • **Monument** (Sonodisc, France)
⚫ *Bantous de la Capitale,* **El Manicero** (Soul Posters, France)
⚫ *Youlou Mabiala,* **The Best of...v. 1 & 2** (Sonodisc, France)
⚫ *Pamelo Mounka,* **Plus Grands Succès** (Karac/Sonodisc, France)
⚫ *Various,* **Musique Congolo-Zairoise, 62-73** (Sonodisc, France)
⚫ *Tchico Tchicaya,* **Full Steam Ahead!** (GlobeStyle, UK)
⚫ *Zao,* **Moustique** (Mélodie, France)

Above: Jean-Serge Essous

KENYA'S BENGA BOOM

In the East African music capital, Nairobi, the African Broadcasting Service once aired a mix of Cuban dance music, early Congo rumba and Zairean finger style guitar, along with South African *kwela* and traditional sounds mostly from Kenya's native Luo and Kikuyu peoples. But after construction of the first Kenyan recording studio in 1947, musicians inevitably set about defining a national sound. By the late '60s, guitar-based bands cranked out Luo songs in an energetic new style called *benga* that thrived for two decades and survives today.

Guitar pickers had long mimicked the quick, syncopated melodies of the Luo's eight-string *nyatiti* lyre. Now, as electric benga emerged, the nyatiti's push-and-pull character also influenced prominent electric bass lines. In benga, the hi-hat sizzles, the bass leaps and voices cry out high-pitched harmonies, while two or three guitars chase each other in sprightly interplay. Born in 1940 in Shirati, Tanzania, the first lord of benga, **Daniel Owino Misiani,** formed his group **Shirati Jazz** in '67 and remained at or near the top through the 1980s. Alternating between ultrafast guitar riffs and lead vocals, Daniel spun out dance hits, but also developed the down-to-earth poetry craved by East African pop fans. His antennae ever honed to popular themes, Daniel mostly sings about love, history and religion, depending on the mood of the moment.

Shirati's toughest competition has come from the **Victoria Kings**—A, B and C versions. Founders **Collela Mazee** and **Ochieng Nelly Mengo** grew up in Kenya near Lake Victoria, in the hot, dry hills that lead south to the Tanzanian border. Born in '54, young Collela had to hide his homemade guitar from disapproving parents. But after he joined

<<The best of Benga from the West of Kenya>>

Nelly to form **Victoria Jazz** in 1972, the pair hit Nairobi in time to bask in the glories of benga's golden age. By the end of the '70s, potent forms of Zairean pop threatened local Kenyan music to the point where Voice of Kenya radio discouraged all but East African pop on the airwaves, boosting benga to new heights. The Victoria Kings' humorous love songs, laced with advice on morality and

good living, outsold other popular benga acts like **George Ramongi, Gabriel Omolo, Sega Sega** and **Ochieng Kabeselleh**.

Now in the age of cassettes, and hence cassette piracy, Kenya's traditionally record-based music scene has flagged. But the music plays on. Fast production times—with songs released in as little as two days—let pop singers converse with the timeliness of news commentators. Meanwhile, neo-traditional groups, notably **Kapere Jazz Band**, formed in 1986, and *nyatiti* player **Ogwang Lelo Okoth** are reviving the Luo roots of benga by returning to the one-string *orutu* fiddle, the nyatiti lyre, as well as Fanta bottle and other percussion.

○ Daniel Owino Misiani and Shirati Jazz, **Benga Blast** (Stern's Earthworks)
○ Daniel Owino Misiani and Shirati Jazz, **Piny Ose Mer: The World Upside Down** (GlobeStyle, UK)
○ The Victoria Kings, **The Mighty Kings of Benga** (GlobeStyle, UK)
○ Kapere Jazz Band & Various, **Luo Roots** (GlobeStyle, UK)

Above: D. O. Misiani

SIMBA WANYIKA, "THE LIONS OF THE SAVANNAH"

Given the strong Zairean influence in East Africa, Kenya naturally produced its share of rumba-oriented groups. Brothers **Wilson** and **George Peter Kinyonga** launched the most successful of these, **Simba Wanyika**, in 1971. They began in their home-town Tanga, Tanzania with the band **Jamhuri Jazz**, which lasted from 1966 to '70. In the early '70s, the brothers went north to Nairobi to form Simba Wanyika. Inspired early on by guitar giant Dr. Nico, Wilson fronted a rich, guitar-driven sound, blending the spare instrumentation of '70s rumba-rock with the gentle rhythms and fullness of older rumba, and warm Swahili vocals. Simba underwent a number of schisms that created a clan of new bands, including **Les Wanyikas**, **Super Wanyikas** and **Wanyika Stars**. In the early '80s, the brothers themselves even split, but soon rejoined to top the charts again with "Shilingi," selling nearly 50,000 legal copies. In 1992, on their 20th anniversary, Simba recorded their first CD, *Pepea*, which served as an international calling card when they became one of the few Kenyan bands to tour in Europe. But sadly, George Peter died of tuberculosis at 42 before the year was out, and today, Simba carries on with Wilson at the helm.

- Simba Wanyika, **Pepea** (Kameleon/Stern's)
- Various, **Kenya Dance Mania** (Stern's Earthworks) • **Guitar Paradise of East Africa** (Stern's Earthworks)

SAMBA MAPANGALA AND VIRUNGA

As the rumba revolution heated up in Kinshasa, Zaire, many talented musicians moved on to spread the rumba gospel. Singer **Samba Mapangala** left Kinshasa in 1975, and went on to become one of the most beloved singers of East Africa. Barely escaping the turmoil of Idi Amin's Uganda, Samba came to Nairobi in '77 and established a successful residency at the Garden Square with his group **Les Kinois**. In 1980, the group broke up and Samba collaborated with Kenyan players to form **Virunga**, named after a volcano in Zaire. Virunga's arrangements feature two free-wheeling saxophones whose lines fatten the sound, weaving with guitar accompaniments behind superb solos by lead guitarist **Rissa-Rissa**. Samba's flawless tenor rises above everything to swoon and cry with the best of the Kinshasans, only now he sings in Swahili as well as Lingala. Virunga's "Malako Disco" stands as one of the biggest dance floor hits Kenya has seen. In 1984, Samba fell foul of the Kenyan government's attempts to boost local music by discouraging the Congolese sound. Refused a work permit, Samba left the country only to return in 1988, his popularity undiminished. His 1991 release *Feet on Fire* epitomizes Kenyan rumba, but also contains a few surprises, like an adaptation of a taarab wedding song, "Vidonge." Other great Kenyan bands lead by Zairean expatriates include **Super Mazembe** and **Les Mangelepa**.

- Samba Mapangala and Orchestre Virunga, **Virunga Volcano** (Stern's Earthworks, UK) • **Feet on Fire** (Stern's Africa)
- Various, **Kenya Dance Mania** (Stern's Earthworks)

Right: Virunga bandsman

LUHYA, KIKUYU AND KAMBA POP

Groups singing in Luhya, Kikuyu and Kamba sweeten Kenya's pop. The nimble sukuti guitar sound of the western Luhya highlands, popularized by '50s stars **George Mukabi** and **John Mwale**, helped define the rhythmic and melodic vocabulary for much electric music that followed. In the '60s, Luhya guitarist and singer **Shem Tube** and his group **Abana Ba Nasery** ("Nursery Boys") recorded hits with dueling acoustic guitars, three-part vocal harmonies, and ringing Fanta-bottle percussion. Shem and his partner **Justo Osala** later formed an electric, benga-oriented band called **Les Bunyore**. Since the '80s, **Sukuma Bin Ongaro** has remained the top electric Luhya star. In an unusual comeback of an all-but-vanished style, Abana Ba Nasery regrouped in 1991 to record acoustically with folk musicians in the UK.

The Kikuyu of Central Province make up Kenya's largest ethnic group, but surprisingly little of their music has percolated beyond the ranks of the Kikuyu. The godfather of Kikuyu pop **Joseph Kamaru** burst onto the scene in 1967 with a Kikuyu take on benga that also nods to country-and-

western music. Kamaru rejects love songs to focus playfully but pointedly on a variety of social topics using masterful "deep Kikuyu," full of proverbs and metaphors. Kamaru's "X-rated, Adults Only" shows remained a draw until he became a born-again Christian in 1993 and embarked upon a new career in gospel. **Peter Kigia and the Chania River Boys** also take on social themes, while **Councilor DK** sings love songs that are popular with the young crowd.

Kamba people inhabit the parched highlands south and east of Nairobi and play music close to the benga/rumba mainstream, but with distinct local melodies. In the '70s and '80s, the Kamba audience favored **Peter Mwambi** and his **Kyanganga Boys**, while **Kakai Kilonzo's Kilimambogo Brothers** sang in Swahili and achieved mainstream success. Having produced a string of Kamba/Swahili crossover hits in the '90s, the **Katitu Boys** now rank as one of the top dance acts in Nairobi.

Left: Joseph Kamaru

⦿ *Abana ba Nasery,* **!Nursery Boys Go Ahead!** (*Xenophile, US/GlobeStyle, UK*) • **Classic Acoustic Recordings from Western Kenya** (*GlobeStyle, UK*)
⦿ *Various,* **Before Benga, V. 1: Kenya Dry** (*Original Music*) • **Before Benga, V. 2: The Nairobi Sound** (*Original Music*) • **The Nairobi Beat: Kenyan Pop Music Today** (*Rounder, US*)

JUWATA JAZZ

In contrast to neighboring Kenya, Tanzania's recording industry remains undeveloped. Groups tape annual sessions at the national radio studio, and make their reputations through frequent live shows. Dance clubs have defined the Dar es Salaam scene since the '30s. Once-private social clubs have evolved into government-run establishments that own P.A. equipment and employ musicians to play up to six nights a week. Formed in 1964 under the auspices of National Union of Tanzania (NUTA), **Juwata Jazz** still draw big crowds, and remain the grandfather of all Tanzania's dance bands. Relaxed grooves, lush horn sections and interlocking guitars mark a rumba influence. But Tanzania's long-standing insistence on local content on the radio has fostered a national sound. Composer and singer **Muhiddin Maalim** helped form Juwata Jazz in '64. After stints with **Mlimani Park Orchestra** and **Orchestra Safari Sound** in the '80s, he now leads Juwata Jazz again. Another Juwata veteran, **Joseph Lusungu** (trumpet and vocals) joined the band along with **Mnenge Ramadhani** (sax) in 1966 and established the group's brass-oriented sound.

In Tanzania, bands adapt one of the traditional ngoma dances as their mtindo, or trademark style. Juwata's mtindo is the drum dance called msondo. The founders of many top groups, including **Mlimani Park**, had their

apprenticeship here, in what remains Tanzania's most durable band.

⦿ *Various,* **Tanzania Dance Bands, V. 1-2** (*Monsun/Line, Germany*)

MLIMANI PARK ORCHESTRA

Dar es Salaam's top band in recent years, **Mlimani Park Orchestra** formed in 1978 and soon dominated the busy dance club scene in the city suburbs. Mlimani Park's extensive radio play, and turnouts of up to 1,000 people at shows testify to their top flight popularity. Radio listeners voted their infectious 1980s hit, "Neema" ("My Comforter"), song of the year. The song typifies the mature, big band sound of Tanzania. Looping around a seductive guitar riff and full-force horn-section blasts, singer **Cosmos Tobias** croons a soaring, lachrymose solo lead. The song's fast dance section mirrors the Zairean *seben*, but with layered horns and tricky guitar picking shot full of traditional Tanzanian rhythms. Mlimani Park's main composer **Hassani Bitchuka** remains one of the country's favorite songwriters because he transforms the events of ordinary life into poetry in the idealistic tradition fostered during the 1960s under President Julius Nyerere. Credit for Mlimani's precise, varied arrangements goes to **Michael Enoch**. Veteran lead guitarist of the '60s-era **Dar es Salaam Jazz Band**, Michael arranges Mlimani's three-guitar juggernaut renowned for producing ecstasy in the open-air dance clubs. These days, Michael plays sax and leads the band's distinctive horn section.

◉ Mlimani Park Orchestra, *Sikinde* (Africassette, US) • *Sungi* (African Music, Germany)

REMMY ONGALA

Born in Kivu, eastern Zaire, **Remmy Ongala** grew up in a musical family during the glory days of Franco's TPOK Jazz. Franco's full, easy sound remained a decisive model as Remmy moved on to Dar es Salaam in 1978 to join his uncle's band, **Orchestra Makassy**. When Makassy went to Kenya, Remmy stayed behind and joined **Orchestre Matimila**, since renamed **Super Matimila**. Remmy's group gets big band textures from the horn section and from elaborate arrangements for three guitars. Remmy calls his music *ubongo*, Swahili for "music of the brain," but it also has heart. Self-appointed spokesman for Dar es Salaam's urban poor, Remmy tackles thorny social and political issues and holds forth in lengthy poetic meditations. In his song "Mambo kwa soksi" ("Things with socks"), Remmy offers a primer on using condoms to protect against AIDS. The song proved too much for Radio Tanzania, which refused to play it. But live shows and black market tapes ensured that few urban Tanzanians missed the message. In the late '80s, Peter Gabriel's WOMAD organization afforded Remmy a unique opportunity to record and perform in Europe. Some observers feel that the experience disrupted Remmy's music, forcing him to slim down his lineup, shorten his shows and favor a more *soukous*-oriented approach. In the process, he's lost musicians and some of his following at home. However the period did yield the particularly beautiful, well-produced *Songs for the Poor Man* and a follow-up *Mambo*.

◉ Remmy Ongala and Super Matimila, **Songs for the Poor Man** (RealWorld, UK) • **Mambo** (RealWorld, UK)
◉ Orchestre Makassy, **Agwaya** (Virgin, UK)

EAST AFRICAN TAARAB

The *taarab* ensembles and orchestras of Swahili-speaking East Africa offer one of the more unexpected sounds in African pop—elegant, sensual compositions filled with poetic nuance and musical virtuosity. Centered in the coastal cities of Tanzania and Kenya, taarab's fusion of Indian, Arabic and African elements has spread beyond local communities to become popular from Mozambique to the Arabian Gulf. The root word of taarab, *tariba*, means "to be moved or agitated." Like much of Swahili culture, taarab began in the Kenyan port of Lamu. After studying there early this century, blind singer and oud player **Mbaruku** helped move the music's creative center south to Mombasa. In the '30s, Mombasa's **Jauharah** and **Morning Star Orchestras** became taarab's first full-sized ensembles.

Swahili *ngoma* or drum song styles like *vugo*, *kumbwaya* and the driving *chakacha* with its sexual overtones—animate most forms of taarab. Egypt's *firquah* film orchestras provided an important model in the '50s, and more recently, Egyptian and Lebanese pop and especially Hindi film pop have influenced taarab melodies and vocal stylings. Taarab groups range from small "parties" to orchestras that can include African drums, tablas, *dumbek* (hourglass drum), *rika* (tambourine), oud (fretless lute), *qanun* (trapeziform plucked zither), *taishokoto* (a banjo-like instrument of Japanese origin with a typewriter-like keyboard used to pluck the strings), as well as organ and accordion. Guitar and bass typically play, but often get overwhelmed by clusters of violins and cellos. Right up front in the sound, male and female vocalists use high, clear-toned voices, Islamic in flavor, but cooler and less wailing than the Muslim singers of North and West Africa.

Taarab songs explore romance and marriage, though their stylized Swahili poetry can suggest political interpretations. During the wedding season in Mombasa, Kenya, people flood the streets coming and going to and from men's and especially women's taarab parties where musicians play styles of music especially suited to each day of the week-long wedding ritual. Kenyan star **Zein L'Abdin,** specializes in the old Lamu style of Swahili taarab. His languid rhythms and floating, world-weary vocals revolve around virtuoso oud flights. But **Maulidi & Musical Party** dominate the Mombasa scene. Formed in 1972 by singer/composer **Maulidi Juma Iha,** this group plays both Hindi pop-oriented tunes and the older Swahili styles. Maulidi records top-selling cassettes with a variety of singers, including local female stars **Malika** and **Zuhura Swaleh**. Maulidi himself shines brightest when singing at a *kutoleza nje*, the all night pre-wedding blast at which women shed their *buibui*, black veils, to reveal elegant dresses, jewelry and henna-decorated hands and feet.

Down on the northern Tanzanian coast, the city of Tanga fostered an influential taarab scene in the '60s. By incorporating dance rhythms, guitars and local folklore, Tanga groups like **Black Star Musical Club** and its spinoff **Lucky Star**, played a strain of taarab that spread to Burundi and Kenya. Further south, in Dar es Salaam **JKT Taarab**'s chakacha-oriented taarab has made them the top orchestra in East Africa. But in 1993, two new outfits

TOT Taarab and **Muungano Taarab** shook things up with a modern, electric sound and provocative lyrics.

At the turn of the century, on the nearby spice island of Zanzibar, Sultan Ali bin Hamoud encouraged the formation of men's social clubs, some of which formed orchestras. Founded in 1905, **Ikwhani Safaa** still supports a 25- to 35-piece group. Then singer **Siti bint Saad**, called the most popular Swahili singer, broke the all-male convention by recording hits up until the '40s. In the '50s, women singers came on strong as groups like **Sahib El-Arry** and **Royal Air Force** reacted against the staid male clubs singing *mipasho* (back-biters) songs. Competition grew so fierce among them that the government formed a national women's group to unite opposing singers. Zanzibar's most renowned orchestra, **Culture Musical Club**, formed in 1958 and received government largesse after the British left Zanzibar in 1964, the beginning of a general era of Africanization.

Taarab groups rarely tour, but an exceptional series of digital field recordings on the British GlobeStyle label presents taarab from Mombasa, Tanga and Zanzibar.

- Maulidi & Musical Party, **Mombasa Wedding Special** (GlobeStyle, UK)
- Zuhura Swaleh w/Maulidi Musical Party, **Jino La Pembe** (GlobeStyle, UK)
- Zein Musical Party, **The Style of Mombasa** (GlobeStyle, UK)
- Culture Musical Club, **Taarab 4: The Music of Zanzibar** (GlobeStyle, UK)
- Ikhwani Safaa Musical Club, **Taarab 2: The Music of Zanibar** (GlobeStyle, UK)
- Various, **Taarab 3: The Music of Zanzibar** (GlobeStyle, UK)
- Black Star and Lucky Star Musical Clubs, **Nyota** (GlobeStyle, UK)
- Various, **Songs the Swahili Sing** (Original Music, US)

Left: Zuhura Swaleh   Above: Zein L'Abdin

WEST AFRICA

Senegalese historian Amadou Hampate Ba wrote that when an African elder dies, a library of knowledge goes with him. The histories of wide-ranging West African empires—Ghanaian (sixth through 11th centuries), Manding (13th and 14th centuries), Songhai (15th and 16th centuries), as well as older Yoruba, Ashanti and other kingdoms—survive mostly in oral forms, such as the songs and recitations of *griots* or *jalis*, traditional praise singers and historians. Thanks to the griots, almost any child in Mali, Guinea, Gambia, Senegal or The Ivory Coast can tell you stories about Soundiata Keita, founder of the Manding Empire over 800 years ago.

Modern West Africa comprises fifteen countries, vast stretches of savanna and desert, jungled mountains, thousands of miles of coastline, and of course, many hundreds of distinct ethnic groups. The influx of Islam and Christianity, and then colonial adventures by France, England and Portugal further complicate the picture of a region that defies easy generalizations. Still, we can say that a respect for history strongly informs the contemporary lives of West Africans, often providing them with a sense of shared legacy that helps to assuage the potentially dangerous national, ethnic and religious divisions.

Music reinforces West African links to the past, and it has also helped the region reach out to the present day world. No other part of Africa has produced so many international stars—**Youssou N'Dour** and **Baaba Maal** from Senegal, **Alpha Blondy** from The Ivory Coast, **Salif Keita** and **Ali Farka Toure** from Mali, **Manu Dibango** from Cameroon, and

King Sunny Adé and **Fela Kuti** from Nigeria. One can scarcely imagine the global rise of Afropop without these artists' contributions. The particular prowess of West African stars on the international scene may have something to do with the region's long-running cultural conversation with the New World. Many argue West Africa nurtured the ancestral seeds of blues, jazz, rock-and-roll and reggae, sounds now known and imitated around the world.

In pre-colonial times, West Africa's political power lay in landlocked empires that controlled overland trade routes to the Mediterranean, notably through the great markets at Djenne and Timbuktu in present day Mali. Coastal cities began as outposts where goods and slaves were sold to seafaring Europeans, who later returned as colonizers, helping to build these cities into the bustling commercial and cultural hubs they are today. For centuries, the slave trade infused New World societies with a powerful dose of African culture. The Yoruba, for example, one of the most developed civilizations of pre-colonial Africa, wound up concentrated in Cuba, Haiti and Brazil, where they still practice and develop their religion and music.

Like many of West Africa's great musical traditions, Yoruba music begins with a con-

versation among drums. Rhythmic patterns and drum timbres act as voices that complement one another and combine into a dense, disciplined and fantastically unified sound. No other region of the continent can rival the force and diversity of West African drumming—Nigeria's rich Yoruba percus-

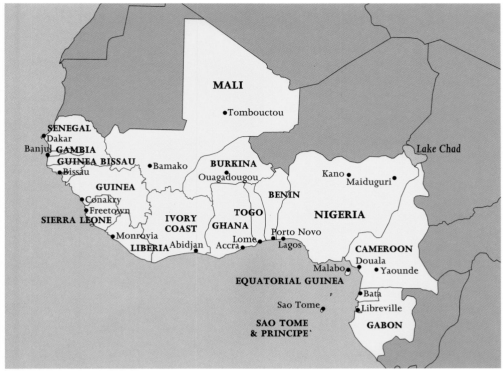

longer, but eventually, musicians there also asserted tradition, developing the dynamic *mbalax* sound that assigned western instruments the roles of drums in a sabar percussion ensemble. Meanwhile, in Ghana and Nigeria, the *highlife* sound that had seduced much of West Africa in the '50s and '60s also gave way to genres with a strong traditional caste, particularly in Nigeria where the ascendant juju and fuji styles put a premium on percussion.

Though West Africans love and revere their musicians, they have not always granted them high social status. A griot may provide the soul of a good wedding party, but he can also be seen as a hustler, and nobody you'd want your daughter to marry. As in other regions of the continent, many a West African star's story begins with the tale of how he or she studied and played music despite parental objections. And frequently, success involved a period of exile. Though Britain and France have long withdrawn from West Africa, their capitals, London and Paris, have provided a vital pathway for musicians in search of an international career. As musicians have moved back and forth, cultural dialogue has continued, and the cities have become important production centers. Meanwhile, West Africa has built up its own studios and production facilities, especially in Lagos, Nigeria, Dakar, Senegal, and Abidjan, Ivory Coast, the region's recording industry capital.

Opposite left: Ibrahima Sylla   Opposite above: Djeneba Diakite and Group   Opposite below: Bouba Sacko Below: Mosque and marketplace, Djenne, Mali

sion, Ashanti and Ewe ensembles from Ghana, *sabar* stick drumming from Senegal, the electrifying masters of the hand-played *djembe* drum of Mali, Guinea, Senegal and other countries, or various versions of the eloquent talking drum, whose tone rises and falls as the player clamps down his arm to squeeze the cords that bind the drum's head to its hourglass-shaped body.

King Sunny Adé's drum-powered juju music sent a wakeup call to the world when he began touring in the early '80s. But many of the West African stars that followed in his footsteps have relied as much on their magnificent voices as on their ancestral rhythms. Baaba Maal describes the Fulani vocal technique called *daandé heli* or "voice exploding," which allows a singer to summon gale force passion and volume. Manding griots have long delivered blasts of vocal power to equal the enormity of the venerable subjects they sing about. With the rise of Latin dance band styles in West Africa, griot singers, and those from other traditions, matched their voices to the popular rhythms of the day, and they have continued to experiment and develop to the point where griot singer and *kora* (21-string harp) player **Mory Kante** produced a disco-fueled dance hit in Europe with his 1988 version of the traditional song "Yeke Yeke."

Since independence, West African countries have all grappled with the problem of revitalizing indigenous ways while engaging the fast-changing world outside. In Mali and Guinea, 1960s-era governments pressed

for the re-Africanization of local music, discouraging popular Latin sounds and ordering bands to adapt folkloric material into their electric pop. As a result, the region's spectacular melodic traditions transformed local dance music. The waterfall melodies of the kora and the wooden-slatted *balafon* turned up in guitar and keyboard parts. The resulting sound, sometimes called Manding swing, won a big audience for state-sponsored dance bands in these countries and laid the groundwork for crossover stars like Salif Keita and Mory Kante. In Senegal, Latin music lasted

YOUSSOU N'DOUR

Senegal's golden-throated pop colossus **Youssou N'Dour** wowed his first audience when he was just twelve, and went on to conquer much of the world with his blend of traditional *sabar* and *tama* drumming, Latin dance music, rock and r&b. Though Youssou's mother came from a *griot* family, his father opposed his son's musical career. But once the Senegalese heard Youssou's majestic voice, life in the civil service was out of the question. In 1979, "Dakar's Little Prince" formed the **Super Etoiles**, and became the most popular singer of Senegal's *mbalax* pop. Youssou soon won the ear of Peter Gabriel, who eventually invited him to join Amnesty International's "Human Rights Now" world tour in 1988. Youssou still works with many of his original musicians, including talking drum master **Assane Thiam**, **Babacar Faye** on sabar drums, and bassist, keyboard player and arranger **Habib Faye**. Softening the jagged sabar rhythms to create savvy, contemporary pop, Youssou sings in five languages to reach the widest possible audience. Some of Youssou's older fans find his new sound too western, but he doesn't mind. "I am a modern man," says Youssou. "I love traditional things, but I think African music must be popular. We have to go forward." Intent on bringing his countrymen along, Youssou recently built a 24-track recording studio called Xippi or "Eyes Open" for musicians in Dakar. Early Xippi releases include work by singer **Manel Diop**, and also Youssou's sister, **Abibatou N'Dour**. In 1994, Youssou's collaboration with American/British hip-hop singer Neneh Cherry—the song "7 Seconds"—sold over 1.5 million copies and won MTV Europe's Best Song award.

⦿ *Set* (Virgin) • *Eyes Open (Xippi)* (Columbia) • *The Guide (Wommat)* (Chaos/Columbia) • *Immigrés* (Stern's Earthworks) • *Nelson Mandela* (Stern's Earthworks)
⦿ *Youssou N'Dour w/Etoile de Dakar (v. 1-7)* (Stern's Africa)

Below: Assane Thiam

ISMAEL LÔ

"I am not a traditional musician," says Senegalese troubadour **Ismael Lô**. Born in 1960, the son of a civil servant, Ismael grew up in a household rocking with soul—Wilson Pickett, James Brown and Otis Redding. He loved the deeply rhythmic *sabar* drumming of the Wolof people as well as the serene textures of the harp-like *kora* and the *balafon*, played by the Manding *griots*. But when he became a musician himself, Ismael's instincts drew him to western instruments—guitar and harmonica. He built his first guitar from a cooking oil can, and learned to play harmonica and guitar together by nailing his harmonica to the wall. In 1979, Ismael first performed his intimate, soulful songs on national television, winning widespread praise. He played for five years in **Super Diamono**, a top *mbalax* band, but then opted for the freedom and flexibility of a solo career. Ismael made a string of successful records with West Africa's premier producer, **Ibrahima Sylla**, and went on to bring his homespun anthems and ballads to an international audience. "My themes concern real life in Senegal," says Ismael. "I speak of racism, poverty, famine and the relationships among people." Ismael sometimes gets overshadowed internationally by the fanfare surrounding Youssou N'Dour and **Baaba Maal**, and **Toure Kunda**, the group that introduced Senegalese pop to Europe in the early '80s. But back home, Ismael, Youssou, and Baaba along with veteran singers **Thione Seck** and **Omar Pene** still make up the top tier of the pop echelon.

⦿ *Natt* (Syllart/Mélodie, France) • *Diawar* (Stern's Africa) • *Tajabone* (Mango, US/Barclay, France) • *Iso* (Mango, US)
⦿ *Omar Pene & Super Diamono*, **Nila** (Celulloid, France) • *Fari* (Stern's Africa)
⦿ *Super Diamono*, **People** (Encore/Mélodie, France)
⦿ *Thione Seck*, **Le Pouvoir d'un Coeur Pur** (Stern's)
⦿ *Toure Kunda*, **The Best of...** (Celluloid, France)

BAABA MAAL

From the northern, riverside town of Podor comes a modern musician filled with the mysteries of ancient Africa. Catlike and delicate in appearance, **Baaba Maal** sings with hurricane force. His music embraces the gentle filigree of West African folk, the tumult of *mbalax* and the toughness of rap and reggae. Baaba comes from the Toucouleur people who live in the Fulani *fouta* region, by the Senegal River, which divides Senegal and Mauritania. Young Baaba left home and moved to the Wolof-dominated capital Dakar to study music and explore his national culture. He soon returned home spent a year with his group traveling along the Senegal River and learning from the old musicians village by village. In 1982, Baaba went to a conservatory in Paris, where he performed with his longtime friend the blind singer **Mansour Seck**. The duo pricked up ears in Europe before going back to Senegal to form Baaba's current group, **Dande Lenol**, or "Voice of the People." The group has played a key role in African pop's incorporation of hip-hop, reggae and techno, notably on their landmark 1994 release, *Firin' in Fouta*. Baaba also maintains an acoustic group that plays and records folkloric music. A true original, Baaba celebrates village life even as he advocates contemporary causes, including women's rights in Africa. Like the griots he admires, Baaba sings of history and heroes,

bringing the lessons of the past into peoples' lives today.

⦿ *Firin' In Fouta* (Mango, US)

⦿ Baaba Maal w/Mansour Seck, *Djam Leelii* (Mango, US)
⦿ Baaba Maal, *Baayo* (Mango, US) • *Lam Toro* (Mango, US) • *Tono* (acoustic, local cassette)
⦿ Mansour Seck, *N'der Fouta Tooro, v. 1* (Stern's Africa)

SENEGAL STAR SEARCH

Senegal hosts one of the most developed West African music industries, and innovative new artists turn up in the cassette stalls of Dakar's crowded markets all the time. Many artists deserve profiles, but here's a quick tour. Young singer **Madou Diabate** has done phenomenally well with serious themes and a trimmed-down, punchy take on *mbalax*. **Super Diamono**'s veteran guitar ace **Lamine Faye**—one of four legendary musical brothers in Dakar—now heads **Lemzo Diamono**, a crossover band with a driving, rock-oriented sound. The top name in Senegalese heavy metal, **Demba Dia**, calls his sound *rock mbalax*—not profound, but a big hit with Dakar youth. Another Super Diamono veteran, percussionist **Thio Mbaye** recently worked with producer Ibrahima Sylla to record the hard-hitting *Rimbax*, which veers between mbalax, traditional *sabar* tracks, and the newly popular Senegalese rap style called *tassou*. **Positive Black Force**, a new tassou group, collaborated with **Baaba Maal** in 1994, and recently signed for an international release with Mango. Once a singer in the innovative '70s band **Xalam**, **Souleymane Faye** now has a strong solo career, and in a departure from the customary standoffishness among competing stars, Souleymane recently collaborated with up-and-coming singers **Cheihk Lô** and **Coumba Gawlo Seck**. Ex-**Super Etoile** drummer **Pape Dieng** has joined the growing ranks of Dakar producers, turning out superior mbalax releases for **Thione Seck** and relative newcomer **Khar M'Baye Maddiaaga**, a female griot singer whose melismatic voice recalls gravel-throated flamenco singers. But despite competition from Khar and Coumba, the grand lady of Senegalese pop remains **Kine Lam**, a booster of traditional culture who roared onto the pop scene in the '80s and now records both acoustic traditional records and state-of-the-art mbalax.

⦿ Xalam, *Xarit* (Jetset, France) • *Gorée* (Celluloid, France) • **Positive Black Force,** forthcoming (Mango, US)

Note: all above mentioned artists are available on local cassettes, available as imports. See Source list on pgs 74-75.

Left: Senegalese percussionist Mor Thiam

SALIF KEITA

In 1968, in the Malian capital of Bamako, a 19-year-old albino boy scrapped the conventions of his noble ancestry to become a professional singer. Poor despite his social standing, rebellious, and vexed by poor eyesight, the boy chose music over the only alternative he saw, a life of crime. **Salif Keita** sang with the legendary, Latin-tinged **Rail Band of Bamako** in the early '70s before starting his own more fusion-oriented group, **Les Ambassadeurs** which also featured brilliant Guinean guitarist **Kante Manfila**. Salif moved to Paris in 1984, and there he recorded *Soro*, a dazzlingly beautiful realization of his brooding, modern take on Malian tradition. *Soro* set a new standard for electric Afropop, and it legitimized African music in the progressive rock mold—music for listening, not just dancing. Salif sings with belting, no-holds-barred passion that evokes blues shouters and r&b screamers. But his sound hews close to the style of the Islamic Manding *griots*, who sing to evoke the grand struggles and tragedies of history. After many struggles, Salif has learned to tap into the pain of life and to transcend it in cathartic song. Today, with a Grammy nomination for his 1992 *Amen*—a collaboration with Weather Report's Joe Zawinul—Salif ranks among the most celebrated African singers who ever lived.

◉ *Salif Keita*, **The Mansa of Mali** (Mango, US) • *Soro* (Mango, US) • **Amen** (Mango, US)
◉ *Les Ambassadeurs Internationales featuring Salif Keita*, self-titled (Rounder, US)
◉ *Les Ambassadeurs*, **Dance Music from West Africa** (Rounder, US)
◉ *Kante Manfila*, **Diniya** (Sododisc, France) • **Tradition** (Celluloid, France) • **Kankan Blues I & II** (PAM Germany)
◉ **Super Rail Band de Bamako** (Indigo, France) • **New Dimensions in Rail Culture** (Globestyle, UK)

AMI KOITA, QUEEN OF THE GRIOT CHANTEUSES

Since ancient times, Manding *griots* have sung histories, lineages and praise songs with grand style and devastating conviction. Of Mali's many *jalimusolu*—female griot singers—none has earned more adulation than **Ami Koita**, a role model for all Mali's contemporary women singers. Ami's big, vibratoless voice and her dazzling lineup of nimble-fingered instrumentalists make her songs of pride, love, tragedy and joy accessible even without translation from her native Bambara. Her traditional acoustic work surrounds her voice with an irresistible chattering of melodies from *balafon* (wooden xylophone), *kora* (21-string harp), *ngoni* (small, banjo-like lute) and guitar, which plays in the lightning quick manner of the other instruments. Recently, Ami has also branched out to record with electric instruments, even collaborating with **Tabu Ley and Afrisa**, one of the great old bands of Zaire. "I am proud to be a griot," sings Ami over the chiming of Zairean guitars. "I become a bird and fly above the people." Brightly-colored traditional gowns spreading wing-like below her gesturing arms reinforce the image, while also reminding audiences that griots are paid well for their praising. Like **Tata Bambo Kouyate**, **Kandia Kouyate, Hadja Soumano, Fanta Naya Diawara** and many other griot chanteuses, Ami provides spiritual advice, musical uplift, and a model of dignity, glamour and poise. In the rough and tumble of Mali's active cassette market, two young Bambara pop singers, **Dieneba Seck** and **Nanou Coul**, have also recently emerged as top sellers.

◉ *Ami Koita*, **Songs of Praise** (Stern's Africa) • **Tata Sira** (Bolibana / Mélodie, France)
◉ *Tata Bambo Kouyate*, **Jatigui** (GlobeStyle, UK)

ALI FARKA TOURE

Now in his fifties, Mali's most famous guitarist **Ali Farka Toure** would happily pass his remaining days tending his farm in the town of Niafounke along the dry northern reaches of the Niger River. But the world's appetite for his warm, spiritual picking and singing won't let him stop. Ali's admirers in the west see him as an African bluesman, a spiritual cousin of John Lee Hooker. But for Ali, American blues presents a New World reflection of Malian sounds he has known all his life. Ali champions the beautiful, old cultures of the Timbuktu region. He says, "The Tamasheck, Peul, Dogon, Songhai, Bambara, Bozo and Maure—seven races, seven different languages. But we live together in Niafounke." When Ali was ten, he started playing the instruments he calls his teachers: a small one-string guitar called *njurkel* and the tiny *njarka* fiddle, a fist-sized gourd with a foot-long neck for its thin gut string. Then he discovered the guitar and began to play it with encouragement from **Fodeba Keita**, founder of Guinea's Ballet Africaine. After touring internationally and recording many records abroad, Ali recently worked with American guitarist Ry Cooder on the Grammy-winning *Talking Timbuktu*, one of the most successful collaborations yet between African and American musicians. Ali recently produced a record for another northern guitarist/singer, **Lobi Traore**. Meanwhile, northern Mali has its pop divas as well, notably **Fissa Maiga** and **Khaira Arby**.

◉ *The River* (World Circuit/Hannibal, UK & US) • *The Source* (World Circuit/Hannibal, UK & US) • *African Blues* (Shanachie) • *Talking Timbuktu (w/ Ry Cooder)* (World Circuit/Hannibal, UK & US)
◉ Lobi Traoré, *Bamako* (Cobalt/Buda, France)

OUMOU SANGARE AND THE WOMEN OF WASSOULOU

The Wassoulou region of southern Mali has earned a reputation for bluesy rhythms and melodies, and stunning, female vocalists. With sculpted braids, flowing robes and an angel's voice, **Oumou Sangare** leads the *Wassoulou* invasion now competing with Mali's once-dominant *griot* music. "People like rhythms that make them move," says Oumou. "When you hear Wassoulou music, you get up and dance." Oumou's mother and grandmother sang, and they encouraged her to do so from the age of five. In 1986, the 18-year-old Oumou toured in the French Caribbean and Europe with a 27-piece folkloric troupe. At 21, she ignited the Wassoulou explosion with her smash debut cassette *Moussoulou* ("Women"), which sold 200,000 legal copies, and many more in the pirate cassette trade. Youth lies at the core of Wassoulou music. Its central instrument, the *kamele ngoni* ("young person's harp") has six strings, a long neck and a calabash resonator. Its larger cousin, the buzzing, boomy *doso ngoni* ("hunter's harp") accompanies the sacred songs hunters use to communicate with their guiding spirits. A rebel for women's causes, Oumou challenges longstanding practices of arranged marriages and polygamy. Musically, though, she sticks to her

roots, rejecting electronic instruments and limiting her sound to kamele ngoni, djembe drum, violin, flute, guitar, bass, the scraped, metallic *karagnan* and her own heart-tugging voice. Among many other women singers currently popular in Mali, **Dieneba Diakite** also favors an acoustic sound, while the gutsy **Coumba Sidibe** and adventurous **Sali Sidibe** put out harder-edged, electric Wassoulou music. An early success with her well-produced '80s Paris releases, **Nahawa Doumbia** still carries the Wassoulou torch as well.

◉ Oumou Sangare, *Moussoulou* (World Circuit) • *Ko Sira* (World Circuit/Rounder)
◉ Nahawa Doumbia, *Mangoni* (Mélodie, France)
◉ Djeneba Diakite, *Piraterie* (Cobalt/Mélodie, France)
◉ Sali Sidibe, *From Timbuktu to Gao* (Shanachie, US)
◉ Various, *The Wassoulou Sound: Women of Mali* and *The Wassoulou Sound: V. 2* (Stern's)

MORY KANTE AND GUINEA'S GRIOT POP

Guinean vocalist and kora player **Mory Kante** spearheaded the "electro-*griot*" sound that hastened the use of keyboards and drum machines in Malian and Guinean pop. Growing up in an old griot family in eastern Guinea, Mory started on *balafon* and then went to Bamako, Mali, to study *kora* during the era of big, state-sponsored folkloric orchestras. There, he wound up taking **Salif Keita**'s job as lead singer for the **Rail Band**. Mory's splendid voice graces the Rail Band's landmark electric version of the griot epic, "Soundiata," which tells the dramatic tale of the first king of the 13th century Manding Empire. In 1981, Mory moved to Paris where he took high-tech Manding pop to new levels. With electronic instruments and a strong horn section to accompany his racing kora lines and august vocals, Mory's 1980s records achieved tremendous popularity throughout West Africa. In 1988, his version of the classic "Yeke Yeke" from the album *Akwaba Beach* even topped charts in Europe, a rare achievement for an African singer. Not for purists, Mory's aggressive

fusion simplifies the dense rhythms of Manding music in favor of a strong backbeat. He uses kora and balafon mostly to color his dance-oriented numbers, not to define them. Perhaps the most successful of all Guinea's griot singers, Mory returns home regularly but continues to live and work in Paris. Back home, popular singers **Kerfala Kante** and the younger **Oumou Dioubate** continue to update the griot pop scene, and a promising new star, **Ibro Diabate** has touched people especially with his songs about modern life. Like Kante, a singer and kora player, **Camara Aboubacar** has proved the latest toast of Conakry's pop scene.

⦿ *Mory Kante*, **Akwaba Beach** (Barclay, France) • **10 Cola Nuts** (Barclay, France) • **N'Diarabi** (Celluloid, France)
⦿ *Kerfala Kante*, **L'Oiseau de Sankara** (Sonodisc, France)
⦿ *Oumou Dioubate*, **Lancey** (Stern's Africa)
⦿ *Ibro Diabate*, **Allah Nana** (Sonodisc, France)
⦿ *Camara Aboubacar*, **Téléphone** (Celluloid / Mélodie, France)

BEMBEYA JAZZ NATIONAL

During the 1960s and '70s, Guinea's all-powerful president Sekou Toure created a system of state-sponsored national orchestras and instructed them to create modern interpretations of the country's folkloric music. Toure's policy of *authenticité* forced bands to meld traditional music with the Cuban styles and Congolese rumba popular at that time. Guitarists learned to echo the fluid melodies of the *kora* and *balafon*. Horn sections harmonized ancient airs. Rhythm sections learned how to make indigenous music danceable, arriving at the sound called Manding Swing. Singers affected the grand vocal dynamics of the *griots*. From the ranks of the **National Orchestra** came supergroups **Keletigui Traore et ses Tambourinis** and **Bala et ses Balladins**. But the great **Bembeya Jazz National** from northern Guinea proved the most popular of the new dance bands. Their success throughout the countries of the old Manding Empire—Mali, Guinea, Gambia and Senegal—legitimized Toure's cultural renaissance. In 1973, after a long run of blockbuster concerts and recordings, Bembeya suffered the loss of its fabulously charismatic lead singer, **Aboubacar Demba Camara** in a car accident in Senegal.

Down, but not out, Bembeya continued until 1991, largely relying on the strength of **Sekou "Diamond Fingers" Diabate**, one of African pop's most innovative guitar virtuosos. Today, a few Bembeya veterans carry on the roots pop tradition, notably singer **Sekouba "Bambino" Diabate**, who has become a major Guinean star, playing with his mostly acoustic ensemble.

Left: Sekou "Diamond Fingers" Diabate

⦿ *Bembeya Jazz National*, **Bembeya Jazz National** (Sonodisc, France) • **Live—10 Ans de Succès** (Bolibana, France) • **Wa Kele** (Esperance, France)
⦿ *Balla et Ses Balladins*, **Reminiscin' In Tempo** with... (Popular African Music, Germany)
⦿ *Sekouba Bambino Diabate*, **Le Destin** (Popular African Music, Germany)

IVORY COAST'S CULTURAL CROSSROADS

Ivory Coast's capital Abidjan offers recording studios, nightlife, and a diverse cultural milieu from which many African artists, including **Salif Keita**, **Mory Kante**, **Mone Bilé** and **Sam Mangwana,** have launched global careers. Abidjan studios, principally the 32-track JBZ, provide the bulwark of the West African recording industry. Meanwhile, the bars of the poor Treichville quarter have nurtured a variety of Ivorian styles and artists. After independence, '60s artists like the harmonizing **Soeurs Comroe** warmed the public up for the fleet, driving *gbegbe* rhythms that became huge in the '70s when artists like **Sery Simplice** and the **Frères Djatys** used them

to fashion modern pop. The grande dame of Ivorian pop, **Aïcha Koné,** began her career secretly, to foil disapproving parents. But she became a star when she matched her elegance, versatility and full-throated alto with the keen pop instincts of West Africa's top arranger, **Boncana Maiga**. Aicha's varied recordings and classy stage show blend *griot* grandeur with polished takes on Ivorian rhythms and pop trends from *soukous* to *zouglou,* the youth music of the '90s. The closest thing yet to a national Ivorian music style, zouglou takes its name from a communal dance, and generally expresses the troubles and aspirations of students. Zouglou's top singer, **Meiway** trades on style and sex appeal while constructing taut, dramatic arrangements that use rock guitar, soukous animation and gushing keyboards to show off his smooth, delicate tenor, often over the *zoblazo* rhythm. The father of Ivorian roots pop **Ernesto Djedje** popularized the fast *ziglibithy* rhythm in the '70s. These days, **Gnaoré Djimi** carries on the roots tradition with his 14-piece *polihet* outfit. Polihet began as a girls' dance, but Gnaore and others have honed it to a smooth, high-tech 6/8 shuffle, with pummeling percussion breaks. A recent surprise group **Le Zagazougou** use accordion and percussion to pump out racing, giddy pop

with a strong acoustic flavor. Ivorian stalwarts like **Nyanka Bell** and newcomers like the footballer/singer **Gadji Celi** stay on their toes to keep up with new developments in this dynamic musical hub.

◗ Meiway, **Meiway** (Sonodisc, France)
◗ Gadji Celi, Espoir (Sonodisc, France)
◗ Zagazougou, **Zagazougou Coup** (Piranha, Germany)
◗ Aïcha Koné and the Alloco Band, **Mandingo Live from Côte D'Ivoire** (Weltmusik, Germany)

Left: Meiway   Below: Gadji Celi

ALPHA BLONDY AND IVORIAN REGGAE

Ivory Coast's brightest star on the international scene, singer and bandleader **Alpha Blondy** put African reggae on the map. Born Seydou Kone in Dimbokro in 1953, Alpha grew up on the Koran and Dioula ethnic tradition, but he also loved '60s rock and soul and started his first group, **Atomic Vibrations,** while still in high school. Alpha went to New York to study at Columbia in 1976, and got swept up in the international reggae scene. Burned by a producer in his first recording project, Alpha returned home and had a nervous breakdown, after which his parents put him in a psychiatric hospital for two years, an experience that failed to quell his musical ambitions. Working with Ghanaian friends, he produced a demo that lead to *Jah Glory,* his unprecedented triple gold debut in 1983. A Muslim and a Rastafarian, Alpha delivers bold political and spiritual messages in Dioula, French and English. His records *Cocody Rock* and *Apartheid is Nazism,* recorded with members of Bob Marley's band,

established him as a West African youth hero and an international star. Today, Alpha lives in France while back home, younger reggae singers create a buzz, notably **Jah Solo Gunt** and **Serges Kassy**.

◗ Alpha Blondy, **The Best of Alpha Blondy** (Shanachie, US) • **Apartheid is Nazism** (Shanachie, US) • **Live au Zenith** (Paris) (World Pacific, US) • **Masada** (World Pacific, US)

E.T. MENSAH AND HIGHLIFE

Highlife, dance music played mostly in Ghana and Nigeria, represents one of the century's first fusions of African roots and western music, and before 1970, it ruled dancefloors across much of West Africa. Trumpeter and bandleader **E.T. Mensah**, born in 1919 in Accra, Ghana, formed his first band in 1930s and went on to be crowned the King of Highlife. The World War II era introduced American swing to the highlife mix, already a blend of Trinidadian calypso, military brass band music, Cuban *son* and older African song forms. In 1948, Mensah formed the **Tempos** whose songs in English, Twi, Ga, Fante, Ewe, Efik and Hausa seduced admirers as far away as England. In 1956, Mensah's career reached a peak when he performed with the great Louis Armstrong in Ghana. With the rise of Congolese music in the 1960s, highlife's golden era ended. But Mensah continued to perform, as did other top big bands, **Jerry Hansen** and his **Ramblers International**, and **Uhuru.** In the Tempos' wake came many guitar highlife outfits, including **Nana Ampadu** and his band the **African Brothers** as well as the **City Boys** and **A.B. Crentsil**. Nana now operates a recording studio where he produces releases for the African Brothers, the City Boys, and other highlife groups. **Dr. K. Gyasi and his Noble Kings** pioneered a sound called *sikyi* highlife, a lulling, wistful take on the classic dance music. Gyasi too still records, as does Kumasi-based sikyi highlife singer **Nana Tuffour.**

○ E.T. Mensah, **All for You** (Retroafric/Stern's) • *Day By Day* (Retroafric/Stern's)
◉ *Tempos/Ramblers/Uhuru,* **Giants of Danceband Highlife** (Original Music, US)
○ *The African Brothers,* **Me Poma** (Rounder, US)
○ *Sweet Talks (w/A.B. Crentsil),* **Hollywood Highlife Party** (Popular African Music, Germany)
◉ *Nana Tuffour,* **Highlife Storm** (Black M Sounds, Germany)
◉ *Various,* **Classic Highlife** (Flying Elephant Records) • *I've Found My Love: 1960's* **Guitar Band Highlife of Ghana** (Original Music, US)

PAT THOMAS AND HIGHLIFE ABROAD

The glory days of *highlife* gave many Ghanaian musicians opportunities to move abroad. In the late '60s, the band **Osibisa** took their "Afro-rock" pop/highlife fusion to a warm reception in England, a harbinger of the world music phenomenon that would explode there a decade later. One of Ghana's most adaptable and popular singers, **Pat Thomas**, has more successfully made the journey from his small town origins to the international crossroads of today's western cities. Pat's career began in 1970 when he joined guitarist **Ebo Taylor's New Broadway Dance Band.** Taylor dismissed Pat as too young until he heard the boy's sweetly melodious voice. Pat went on to score a number of hits with bands he founded, **Sweet Beans** and **Marijata**. Marijata merged highlife and reggae during the late '70s prime of Bob Marley and the Wailers. In 1980, Pat became the first major Ghanaian musician to record in Hamburg, Germany. Pat's musicians used keyboards and elements of the then-popular disco sound to pioneer *burgher highlife*, which overtook guitar highlife during the '80s. Pat moved on to the Ghanaian expatriate community in Toronto, Canada, where he still records. Unlike many African artists who leave home, Pat remains popular in Ghana where many bands

still cover his soul-tinged hits like "Sika Ye Mogya," and "Olivia." Meanwhile, Pat's lead guitarist **George Darko** stayed in Germany to become the first big burgher star. More recently, a young singer called **Daddy Lumba** made his name in the German burgher scene, but now spends half his time in Ghana where his blend of highlife, hip-hop and dancehall reggae has earned him a strong youth following.

○ *Pat Thomas,* **Dancing Time** (Nakasi, UK) • *Sankofa* (Nakasi, UK)
◉ *Osibisa,* **The Best of Osibisa** (KWest)
◉ *George Darko,* **Highlife in the Air** (Hansa, Germany) • **Highlife Time** (Oval, UK)
◉ *Daddy Lumba,* **Playboy** (Black Market Records, Germany)

Above: George Darko

GHANA, THE CONTEMPORARY SCENE

Today Accra moves mostly to the sounds of gospel *highlife*, local reggae and American black pop, while guitar highlife enjoys something of a resurgence. Hard economic times and political instability in the '80s engendered a surge of religious activity, and both resources and artists shifted from nightclubs to churches. The gospel cassette market boomed, and today represents a significant sector in the pop music market with big-selling acts like **Carlos Sekyi,** the **Tagoe Sisters** and **Naana Frimpong**. Reggae has also grown steadily more popular since the '70s, encouraging highlife groups to cross over. Singing in the Twi language, "hitmaker" **K.K. Kabobo** has done well with his gruff voice and his blend of highlife and reggae. A veteran of the band **Classique Vibes,** singer **Kojo Antwi** now sports dreadlocks and outsells all other Ghanaian reggae acts with his easygoing love songs. His recent cassettes have topped 100,000 copies, a high number even in Ghana where government measures have largely curtailed cassette piracy. Guitar highlife remains extremely popular in Ghana's rural areas where "concert parties" combine music and theater in exuberant celebration that can last until sunrise. **Amakye Dede** leads Ghana's top highlife act today. Like most highlife bands, Amakye works the concert party circuit, but he also runs a nightclub, the Abrantee Night Spot, one sure source for live highlife in Accra. Aside from popular foreign-based highlife acts like **Daddy Lumba** and **Pat Thomas,** highlife veterans like **Jewel Ackah** and **A. B. Crentsil** remain active, and new singers like **Sammy Orusu** continue to emerge. A group called the **Western Diamonds** has been voted the best highlife big band in Ghana at the past three GBC (Ghana Broadcasting Company) MUSIGA Awards.

⊙ *Amakye Dede,* **Me Fre Wo** *(Kotoko Records, UK)*
⊙ *Western Diamonds,* **Diamonds Forever** *(Westline/Nakasi, UK)*
⊙ *Jewel Ackah and the Butterfly 6,* **Butterfly 6**
⊙ *A.B. Crentsil,* **Best of Ghana Highlife** *(World Art & Music, UK)*
⊙ *Carlos Sekyi,* **Yesu Christo** *(Megastar, Ghana)*
⊙ *Tagoe Sisters,* **Manya Yesu** *(Megastar, Ghana)*
⊙ *A.B. Crentsil,* **Santana**

CESARIA ÉVORA, CAPE VERDEAN DIVA

More than half of Cape Verdeans live far from the beautiful archipelago their ancestors once called home. The Portuguese discovered these ten Atlantic Ocean islands in 1460, populated them with Africans and Europeans, and governed harshly until 1975. Three-hundred-and-fifty miles off the coast of Senegal, Cape Verde served as one of Africa's first slave ports, and became one of its last nations to achieve independence. All this helps to explain why the melancholy *morna,* an often minor-key song style tied to love, loss and sadness, best expresses the Cape Verdean national identity. And nobody sings a morna with more gusto than **Cesaria Évora**. Cesaria began performing in her teens on the island of Sao Vicente, but she was well into her forties when she went to Paris and received the international acclaim she now enjoys. Known as the "barefoot diva," Cesaria has always performed shoeless, originally because she couldn't afford shoes, and now just because she feels more comfortable that way. Fond of whisky and cigarettes, and a veteran of three marriages, Cesaria's blues have personal as well as cultural roots. She favors an elegant, acoustic backing band—mostly plucked strings—and sings in a robust alto that lifts the weight of hard experience with resolve and tenderness. Cape Verde has also produced many dance pop bands, updating the strongly African *coladeira, funana, bandera* and *batuco* rhythms. The oldest and best

known of these groups, **Os Tubarões,** has performed for nearly three decades. A younger band with a growing international profile, **Finaçon,** takes its name from the improvised chanting style that accompanies the batuco rhythm. Finaçon plays a Paris-preened roots style they call *funacolo*.

⊙ *Cesaria Évora,* **Miss Perfumado** *(Lusafrica/Mélodie, France)* • **Mar Azul** *(Lusafrica/Melodie, France)* • **Le Diva aux Pieds Nus** *(Buda Musique, France)* • **Cesaria** *(Lusafrica, France)*
⊙ *Finaçon,* **Funana** *(Mélodie, France)* • **Simplicidade** *(Mélodie, France)*
⊙ *Os Tubaroes,* **Portons D'Nós Ilha** *(Lusafrica, France)*

KING SUNNY ADÉ

Nigeria's **King Sunny Adé** and his 20-piece **African Beats** hypnotize audiences with juju—deeply layered, percussive groove music. Juju started in the '20s as local bar music and developed over the years absorbing new technologies and influences. In the '50s, amplification made it possible to combine acoustic elements, such as guitar melodies and solo singing from the older *palm wine* music, with full-force ensemble Yoruba drumming to create the rich, dense sound of modern juju. The top ambassador of *juju*, King Sunny Adé sparked an international Afropop invasion with his sensational tours in the early 1980s. KSA, as Nigerians know him, was just 17 when he eluded the expectations of his courtly family to pursue music playing in Lagos *highlife* bands. Soon, he latched on to the juju craze, forming his first band the **Green Spots** in '67. The group emulated the style of juju elder statesman **I.K. Dairo and his Blue Spots**, but by the time KSA launched the African Beats in '74, he had overshadowed Dairo and gone head-to-head with **Chief Commander Ebenezer Obey**. KSA, with his percussive *synchro* system, and Ebenezer, with his melodious *miliki* system, drove juju music to unprecedented heights as they competed to update the sound. Ebenezer introduced the three-guitar lineup and the trap drums; KSA overlaid a pedal steel guitar, and later synthesizers. But juju's core rested in percussion topped by eloquent talk-ing drums, and in harmonized call-and-response vocals mixing Yoruba proverbs and Christian themes. KSA has a gentle, silky voice and diving, birdlike dance moves, which his four backup singers follow as part of the group's masterful stage choreography. With a tilt of his guitar, KSA damps his musicians down to a tap and a whisper, only to have them surge on cue with a rally of drums, shakers, bells and tangling guitars. KSA's 70 records include three pioneering international releases on Island, notably his 1982 international calling card, *Juju Music*.

⊙ *King Sunny Adé*, **Juju Music** (Island) • **Synchro System** (Island) • **Aura** (Island) • **Chuck E** (Sunny Adé, Nigeria)
⊙ *Ebenezer Obey*, **Solution** (Stern's) • **Juju Jubilee** (Shanachie, US)
⊙ *I.K. Dairo*, **Ashiko** (Xenophile, US) • **Juju Master I.K. Dairo MBE** (Original Music, US) • **I Remember** (Music of the World, US)
⊙ *Various*, **Juju Roots** (Rounder, US)

"SIR" SHINA PETERS: JUJU AND BEYOND

After the long, virtually unchallenged reign of King Sunny Adé and Ebenezer Obey, master showman **"Sir" Shina Peters** opened the door to a new generation of juju musicians. He and singer **Segun Adewale** started out backing juju veteran **Prince Adekunle**, but in 1977, Shina and Segun formed **Shina Adewale and the Superstars International**. In 1980, the two young rebels went different ways, Segun promoting a fusion style he called *yo-pop*, and Shina emerging in the late '80s with his Afro-juju style, a more percussion-heavy take on the juju sound. Shina's music nods to Fela Kuti's funky *afrobeat* and to the percussion frenzy of fuji music, but it remains essentially juju. With songs stressing moral themes, Shina has won awards in Nigeria in 1989 and '90. Time will tell if "Shinamania" lasts, but for now, Shina has defined the cutting edge and competitors have followed closely. Meanwhile **Dele Taiwo** makes hay with a punchy, keyboard-rich sound he calls funky juju.

Internationally acclaimed singer **Majek Fashek** heads up the frontline of a Nigerian reggae invasion. With four cassettes on the market, **Ras Kimono**'s good-timing reggae has followed Majek's lead, earning him an audience up the West African coast in Ghana and beyond.

⊙ *Sir Shina Peters*, **Shinamania** (Sony, Nigeria/Flame Tree, UK) • **Afro-Juju 1** (Sony, Nigeria) • **Experience** (Sony, Nigeria/Flame Tree, UK)
⊙ *Segun Adewale*, **OjoJe** (Rounder, US) • **Yo Pop** (Stern's, UK)
⊙ *Majek Fashek*, **Spirit of Love** (Interscope, US)
⊙ *Sonny Okosun*, **Fire In Soweto** (Oti, UK) • **Liberation** (Shanachie, US)
⊙ *Majek Fashek*, **The Best of Majek Fashek** (Flame Tree, UK)

Left: Majek Fashek

CHIEF ALHADJI SIKURU AYINDE BARRISTER

Below: "Spraying" at Barrister show

During the '80s, while King Sunny Adé was bringing *juju* music to the world, the popular *fuji* sound surged to squeeze out an equal share of Nigeria's massive pop market. All percussion and vocals, this Yoruba pop came dramatically to prominence with another great Nigerian musical rivalry, this time between bandleaders **Sikuru Ayinde Barrister** and **Kollington Ayinla**. Barrister, who remains on the leading edge, started out in 1965 singing *were*—songs used to rouse Muslims early in the morning during the holy season of Ramadan. He went on to mix in aspects of *apala* percussion and vocal songs and brooding, philosophical *sakara* music and emerged with a new style of music

he dubbed fuji. Barrister cemented his preeminence with his "fuji garbage" song series. The term played on black American slang where "bad" means "good." It also deflated his critics by insulting the music before they could. Nigerians loved it. Barrister has toured internationally, but mostly plays to all Nigerian crowds. Nigerian audiences often venture onstage to present musicians with bills, or even fistfulls of cash, a practice called *spraying* or *dashing*. At Barrister shows, spraying reaches new heights of showmanship, and the take can be as high as $10,000—impressive, but still not up to King Sunny Adé's level. Barrister toured extensively in 1994, reportedly out of fear that he might be detained if

he went home. His feisty cassette "The Truth" recounted the story of the annulled 1993 elections, and offered a harsh critique of the Nigerian military, which has ruled the country for 24 out of 34 years since independence.

⊙ Barrister, **New Fuji Garbage** (GlobeStyle, UK) • **The Truth** (local cassette) • **Fuji Garbage, Series I, II, III** (cassettes) • **Fuji New Waves** (cassette)
⊙ Kollington Ayinla, **Ijo Yo Yo** (Kollington, Nigeria)
⊙ Various, **Yoruba Street Percussion** (Original Music, US)

ADEWALE AYUBA AND THE NEW FUJI GENERATION

Younger fuji musicians continue to emerge and do well even as juju persists, and reggae makes strong inroads on the Nigerian scene. **Abass Akande Obesere** has recently emerged as a top contender, spicing his songs with obscene lyrics that young Nigerians love. Another up-and-coming fuji star, **Sunny Tua** (a.k.a. **Sunny T.**) had great success with his first release and now finds himself in demand for club shows. Most fuji musicians are Yoruba, but Sunny is Ibo, from the Rivers state in southeast Nigeria. While still young, he moved to the Lagos suburb of Ajegunle and he now incorporates much of the urban slang he learned there into his upbeat songs. Probably the top name in fuji after **Barrister** and **Kollington**, singer

Adewale Ayuba has recorded internationally, touring in the US in 1993. His show features an orchestra of percussion, powerhouse chorus vocals, and dance moves bursting with youth energy. Since his triumphant return, Adewale shows off his newfound passion for an American pastime, pool. He racks up a few games (mostly losing) every Sunday before his weekly show at the Lagos club, Skindles. Other fuji artists of note include **Easy Kabaka**, **Ejire Bonanza** and **Wasiu Ayinde Marshal** with his *talazo* style.

⊙ Adewale Ayuba, **Mr. Johnson** • **Bubble** (Flame Tree/Stern's, UK)

FELA ANIKULAPO KUTI

ew Afropop stars dare use celebrity to criticize political leaders. Of those who have, none has inveighed with such gusto, or paid so dearly for it as Nigeria's maverick bandleader **Fela Anikulapo Kuti**. Born in 1938 to a wealthy family steeped in colonialism, Fela rebelled against his strict upbringing leaving medical school to study music in London during the late '50s. A stay in the US in the '60s nurtured his radicalism, and he went home in 1970 determined to speak out for West Africa's oppressed urban poor. Since then, Fela has led his sprawling, 30-plus-piece *afrobeat* band through scathing broadsides against his government, international business and corrupt leaders all over. Early songs like "Zombie," a swipe at Nigerian Army soldiers, and "International Thief Thief" horrified authorities and earned Fela harsh retribution. In 1977, during the army's second armed march on Fela's communal compound, 1,000 soldiers burned buildings and equipment, brutalized Fela's followers and musicians and threw his 84-year-old mother from a window, hastening her death. Fela's subsequent marriage to 27 women, those loyal enough to stay with him, fortified his regal image, though he later divorced them following his 18-month prison term on trumped-up currency charges. On stage, Fela leads his band through lengthy African funk epistles. While drummers and guitarists etch the groove, Fela preaches in pidgin English, building the feeling with a keyboard break or a blast on his tenor sax. When the song crests, a row of women dance and sing and the band's massive cluster of horns blares out with indignation. The disciplined barrage of Fela's band invites comparisons with James Brown, to which Fela's responds, "I don't object to what people hear. But my music is African music." Fela's son **Femi Kuti**, who led the band during Fela's incarceration, now carries on the afrobeat tradition with his popular 17-piece group, **Positive Force**.

◉ *Fela, Zombie* (Celluloid, US) • ***Black Man's Cry*** (Shanachie, US) • ***Fela*** (Baya, France) • ***Original Sufferhead*** (Shanachie, US) • ***Army Arrangement*** (Celluloid, US)
◉ *Femi Kuti, **Femi Kuti*** (Tabu/Motown, US)

NIGERIAN HIGHLIFE

eginning in the '60s, guitar *highlife* bands grew out of older acoustic "Ibo blues" and *palm wine* music. As in Ghana, the guitar-based sound caught on as a more rock-informed alternative to the big band style pioneered by **E.T. Mensah, Bobby Bentsen** and **Cardinal Jim Rex Lawson.** Bobby and Jim Rex's bands blazed the homegrown highlife trail in Nigeria, starting in the '50s. In 1976, following the end of Nigeria's civil war, **Prince Nico** and his **Rocofil Jazz** scored a huge hit with "Sweet Mother," reportedly the biggest-selling African record ever at over 13 million copies. Half Cameroonian, Nico sought an international sound influenced by Congolese music, and he remained popular into the '80s, though he never recorded a tune to top his early hit. Most of Nigeria's highlife groups came from Iboland, and highlife all over Nigeria remains primarily an Ibo music. Highlife greats include **Chief Stephen Osita Osadebe, Oliver de Coque, Muddy Ibe,** and the legendary **Oriental Brothers**. Originally three actual brothers from the eastern city of Owerri, the Oriental Brothers thrived in the '70s with their complex, buoyant, guitar-and-percussion sound and crying vocal harmonies. Feuds between the brothers ultimately led each to form his own band. Singer **Dr. Sir Warrior** headed one version of the Oriental Brothers, while guitarist **Dan Satch** headed another, and the third brother **Godwin Kabaka Opara** started his own group **Kabaka International.** Highlife goes on, especially in eastern Nigeria, though on the national scene, it remains overshadowed by widely popular juju, fuji and now reggae. One of the first Nigerian musicians to add reggae to the mix, Ibo highlife innovator **Sonny Okosun** still sells well. Sonny began mixing highlife and reggae in the style he called *ozzidi* back in the mid '70s. In 1994, his gospel release *Songs of Praise* sold close to a million copies.

◉ *Prince Nico, **Aki Special*** (Rounder, US)
◉ *Oriental Brothers, **Heavy On the Highlife*** (Original Music, US)
◉ *Chief Stephen Osita Osadebe, **People's Club Special*** (Stern's) • ***Kedu America*** (Xenophile, US)
◉ *Oliver de Coque, **Ogene Super Sounds*** (OGRPLS, Nigeria)
◉ *Various, **Azagas & Archibogs: The Sixties Sound of Lagos Highlife*** (Original Music, US)

ANGELIQUE KIDJO

The music of **Angelique Kidjo**—the queen of African crossover pop—has invited comparisons with Grace Jones, Tina Turner and Chaka Khan. Indeed, her explosive stage energy, razor sharp voice, and fearlessly funky dance pocket puts her in a camp with these divas of western pop, but Angelique rankles at the oft-heard criticism that she has abandoned her African roots. She grew up in Benin, a sliver-like West African nation that marks a crossroads between the Islamic civilizations that came from the north and the older, black African cultures. Her village, Ouidah, lies in a region steeped in traditional African religion, and she still returns there for inspiration. Raised in an artistic family, Angelique sang rock and r&b with her musician brothers before moving to Paris in 1983. There, she lent her voice and percussion prowess to various jazz and pop projects, including Archie Shepp's 1988 *Mama Rosa*. In 1991, she worked with Miami producer Joe Galdo to create *Logozo*, the record that launched her worldwide career and earned her commercial radio play in the US. Fiercely committed to musical adventurism and to the cause of human rights, Angelique sails the most progressive currents in today's Afropop, and reserves choice words for those

who find her slick sound un-African. "The world is getting smaller and smaller," she says. "I sing about problems that are not only in Benin or Africa. I write for everybody."

⊙ Angelique Kidjo, **Parakou** (OMD, France) • **Logozo** (Mango, US) • **Ayé** (Mango, US)

S.E. ROGIE AND PALM WINE MUSIC

With the death of Sierra Leone's **S.E. Rogie** in 1994, the sweet, old West African tradition of *palm wine* guitar has few great players left. In Ghana, **Daniel** "Koo Nimo" Amponsah still picks out the lilting palm wine melodies, but people see him as a preservationist, and few young musicians have picked up the style. Palm wine music dates back to the days when Portuguese sailors first introduced guitars to West African port cities. Early African guitarists and bottle percussionists played at gatherings where revelers drank the fermented sap of palm trees, a traditional alternative to bottled beer. Rogie, palm wine music's greatest ambassador, began his career as "The Jimmy Rodgers of Sierra Leone." His early hit "My Sweet Elizabeth" stands as the most popular song Sierra Leone has produced to date. After he left home in 1973, Rogie's long, up-and-down career took him around West Africa, to the US, and ultimately to England, where he recorded, taught, and performed vigorously until his sudden death at the age of 68. Fortunately, he left behind some fine recordings of his easy, delightful songs, including the ironically titled *Dead Men Don't Smoke Marijuana*, made just months before his own demise.

Left: S. E. Rogie

⊙ S.E. Rogie, **The Palm Wine Sounds of S.E. Rogie** (Stern's) • **Dead Men Don't Smoke Marijuana** (RealWorld, UK)
• Koo Nimo, **Osabarima** (Adasa Records/Stern's)

MAKOSSA'S MARCH

In the 1950s, before Cameroon rallied around its homegrown *makossa* sound, the port city Douala moved to Nigerian *high-life*, Congolese *rumba* and Cuban music. But in the streets, troupes played a spirited folk music called *ambasse bey*, featuring stick-and-bottle percussion and guitar, a sound later popularized by **Salle John**. Guitar-picking singers like **Lobe Rameau** performed and recorded topical songs, but it took **Eboa Lotin**'s guitar-and-harmonica-based releases in the early '60s to bring these elements together and etch the beginnings of a new national sound, named for a children's hand-clapping game, *kossa*. **Misse Ngoh**, guitarist for **Los Calvinos**, moved makossa forward by developing the crisp, circular fingerpicking that became one of its trademarks. Rudimentary two-track recordings made in Douala prevailed until makossa pioneer **Ekambi Brillant** went to Paris and recorded in a modern studio.

By the 1980s, guitarist **Toto Guillaume** and bassist **Aladji Touré** had set up shop in the French capital, arranging and producing a stable of musicians who would shape the gleaming Paris recordings of makossa's hey-day. Singers like **Dina Bell, Guy Lobé, Ben Decca, Manulo, Douleur** and **Pierre De Moussy** fashioned repeating hook melodies, mostly in the Douala language, backed by horn sections and dulcet female chorus singers, notably **Sissy Dipoko, Marilou** and **Francis Titty**. Like the nation's favorite beverage, champagne, makossa delivers sweet, fizzy intoxication. Makossa producers mixed the music's active bass lines loud for a punchy dancehall sound. **Moni Bilé** proved one of the biggest hit-makers, starting with "Bijou" in 1982. But **Sam Fan Thomas**, with a sound based on the faster *makassi* rhythm of western Cameroon, gave makossa its most enduring hit with "African Typic Collection" in 1984. Since his late '60s work with the **Black Tigers**, Sam had worked his way into the Douala makossa scene. "African Typic Collection" celebrated the country's traditional music and worked around a lyrical refrain that proved irresistible and helped spread makossa to other African countries and to the West Indies. Sam's big hit also proved a tough act for him to repeat, and since then, a succession of singers have enjoyed their turn in the spotlight. **Lapiro de Mbanga**'s blend of makossa and soukous proved a marketing master stroke and appealed to a wide audience. Lapiro often sang in pidgin English—understood by more Camerooneans than the Douala language of most makossa hits—and he generated additional excitement with timely political jabs in his lyrics. Meanwhile, new artists like **Charlotte Mbango, Prince Eyango** and **Grace Decca** emerged from the Paris scene. By that time, producers like Toto and Aladji had begun blending makossa with another popular party-hardy style, *zouk* from the French Antilles. The resulting sound, sometimes called *makozouk*, still registers on international dance charts in the wake of the makossa explosion. Singers **Guy Lobé** and **Petit Pays** have had particular success with the makozouk formula.

Makossa veterans have continued to branch out. The great Paris horn section **Jimmy and Fredo** worked out of Washington, DC in the late '80s. More recently, Cameroonian session players, mostly based in Paris, have played key roles in jazz violinist Jean-Luc Ponty's *Tchokola* project, and in Paul Simon's *Rhythm of the Saints* band, which also featured Cameroon's maverick guitarist **Vincent Nguini.**

- *Various,* **Makossa Connection, V. 1-4** (TJR Music/Sonodisc, France)
- *Guy Lobé & Jo Doumbé,* **Top Makossa** (TJR Music/Sonodisc, France)
- *Eboa Lotin,* **Anthologie, V. 1** (Sonodisc, France)
- *Moni Bilé,* **10th Anniversaire: Best of...** (Sonodisc, France)
- *Ben Decca,* **Greatest Hits**
- *Prince Ndedi Eyango,* **You Must Calculer** (Tougata, France)
- *Guy Lobé,* **Mon Amie A Moi** (Toure Jim's, France) • **Union Liberé** (Tougata, France)
- *Lapiro de Mabanga,* **No Make Erreur** (Stern's)
- *Grace Decca,* **Doi la Mulema** (Sonodisc, France)
- *Charlotte Mbango,* **Konkai Mokossa** (Sonodisc, France)
- *Sam Fan Thomas and Charlotte Mbango,* **The African Typic Collection** (Stern's Earthworks)
- *Sam Fan Thomas,* **Makassi** (Tam/G.K./Simba, France) • **Si Tcha** (Sonodisc, France)
- *Ekambi Brillant,* **The Best of Ekambi Brillant: Meilleurs Makossa** (TJR Music/Sonodisc, France)
- *Various,* **L'Age D'or** (TJR/Sonodisc, France)

Above: Sam Fan Thomas

MANU DIBANGO

The nomadic ways of Cameroon's best known maestro **Manu Dibango** have filled his life with auspicious encounters. Born in 1933, Manu went to Paris at fifteen to study. Though his Protestant parents objected, Manu pursued music vigorously, moving from classical piano to saxophone in 1954. He got his first job playing piano with **Francis Bebey,** Cameroon's brilliant writer, musicologist and performer. Manu soaked up the jazz scene in Brussels before moving to Kinshasa, Zaire in 1961, just as the Congolese *rumba* revolution hit its stride. He stayed two years, recording 100 singles with **Joseph Kabesele**'s legendary **African Jazz.** Working between Paris and Douala, Manu then tried his hand at Cameroon's beloved *makossa* music, but also explored a new love, American soul. He married the two styles in his 1973 release "Soul Makossa," a surprise hit in Europe and America that sold more copies worldwide than any prior African single. With his band the **Makossa Gang,** Manu finished out the '70s recording in New York, Lagos, Abidjan, Paris and in Kingston, Jamaica, where he worked with reggae's top rhythm section Sly

and Robbie. Having toured much of the world and experimented with every pop style that interested him, Manu reconnected with jazz in the '80s. In 1985, he brought an array of African stars together to record "Tam Tam pour L'Ethiopie," to raise money to fight that country's famine. During the '90s, Manu has embraced hip-hop and rap, and in 1994, he released *Wakafrika,* guest-spotting a wide range of African star singers to create new interpretations of the continent's pop classics. A universalist not confined to any country or stylistic niche, Manu's adventurism puts him beyond the tastes of most folks back home. In all these years, he's had very few dance hits in Cameroon.

⦿ *Manu Dibango,* **Soul Makossa** • **Seventies Manu Dibango** (Soul Paris/Sonodisc, France) • **Live '91** (Soul Paris/WMD, France) • **Wakafrika** (Giant, US)
⦿ *Francis Bebey,* **1962-1994: Nandolo** (Original Music, US) • **Akwaaba** (Original Music, US)

BIKUTSI POP

In rural Cameroon, acoustic groups playing folkloric *assiko, mangambe* and *bikutsi* music worked the town bar-rooms in the days before the *makossa* boom. Bikutsi, the frenetic roots music of the Beti people around the city of Yaounde, has now developed into an electric sound that rivals makossa. But bikutsi pop dates back to the '40s when veteran singer **Anne-Marie Nzie** first recorded. **Messi Me Nkonda Martin** and his band **Los Camaroes** then pioneered electric bikutsi in the '60s and '70s using keyboards and guitars to play the quick balafon melodies of the traditional music. Whenever these groups played, wild and sexually suggestive dancing ensued. "Bikutsi was bar music," recalls international radio personality Georges Collinet, originally from Cameroon. "There were a lot of small orchestras here and there, and most of them were drunk for their performances. The basic group had three or four *balafons* and drums, and the music had that deep forest, primeval sound." **Les Vétérans** also played a major role in popularizing bikutsi. But the outside world discovered bikutsi when media-savvy journalist and

advertising student **Jean Marie Ahanda** launched the **Têtes Brûlées** in 1987. With colorfully painted bodies, torn clothing, and partially shaved heads, the group combined the music's spikey, bucking rhythms with a space-age image. In 1988, the group weathered the suicide of their original guitarist, **Zanzibar,** who innovated the trick of damping the strings with a strip of foam rubber to produce the music's characteristic balafon-like thunk. Though the Têtes Brûlées still corner the bikutsi market abroad, they get stiff competition back home from rougher-edged outfits led by singers like **Mbarga Soukous** and **Jimmy Mvondo Mvelé.**

⦿ *Les Veterans,* **Au Village, V. 1-3** (Safari Ambiance, France)
⦿ *Les Têtes Brûlées,* **Hot Heads** (Shanachie, US) • **Bikutsi Rock** (Shanachie, US)
⦿ *Tom Youms and the Star's Collection,* **Sunny Days** (TJR, France)
⦿ *Georges Seba,* **Lions Indomptables** (Sonodisc, France)

Left: Les Têtes Brûlées

NORTHERN AFRICA

Often overlooked in discussions of African music, the countries of northern Africa link the continent to the Mediterranean world, and particularly to the rest of the Arabic-speaking world, which at over 200 million people, makes up one of the largest regions on earth to share a common culture and language. The story of North Africa's recording industry begins in Cairo, Egypt, where the Odeon label started up in 1904, producing over 400 titles before World War I. Given Cairo's continuing dominance as a music center, a thumbnail sketch of northern Africa's modern music naturally starts there.

In the grand halls of Cairo today, large *firquah* orchestras combine western and Middle Eastern classical instruments, playing music that carefully preserves and extends centuries-old traditions. The scales, or *maqam*, and forms used in this music, and the time-honored themes in the classical poetry that singers interpret—all exemplified in the works of singer and legend **Oum Kalsoum**—may seem rarefied upon first listen. But for Arabic-speaking peoples, deeply concerned with their history, both the music and the words resonate in ways that have no exact parallel in the western world. Meanwhile, in Cairo's modern recording studios, young pop singers and high-tech troubadours from the city's blue-collar neighborhoods pour their hearts out in plain-spoken, topical confession and complaint. Both Cairo's venerable traditions and its earthy modern pop hold sway over musicians and audiences across the Maghreb, the region that stretches from Libya to the Atlantic, to include Tunisia, Algeria and Morocco—the country known to Arabs as Maghreb Al Aqsa, the extreme west—then south across the Sahara to the Senegal River.

Arab classical music begins with singing, the human voice, a fact that helps account for the amazingly controlled vocal techniques—from delicate whispers to quivering, swooping wails—found in North African music. The singer's art focuses on the interpretation of a text. Vocal techniques serve to amplify and color various levels of meaning in the words. Instrumental improvisation parallels this process as virtuosos playing the *nay*, *qanoon* or *oud*—ancestors of the European flute, zither, and lute respectively—explore the possibil-

ities inherent in a particular scale or composition. Double-reed instruments such as the oboe-like *mizmar baladi* produce an evocative range of vibrant, shrill tonalities. The region's most popular percussion instruments—the frame drum, sometimes called *tar* or *bendir*, and the goblet-shaped *derbouka*—give many styles of music a sensuous undertow that reminds us that Arab percussion is an ancestor of the world's great Latin styles. Various bells, chimes, and castanets ornament some traditional styles, reflecting musical input from the Middle East and beyond.

Northern African music also includes elements of sub-Saharan traditions. The dense rhythms and deep trance incantations of Morocco's Gnawa brotherhood offers one striking example, but the African element can often turn up neatly integrated within otherwise Arab sounds—a particular 6/8 rhythm, an old traditional melody, or a call-and-response vocal or instrumental arrangement.

As elsewhere in Africa, religion and colonialism complicate the story of today's music. Orthodox Islam has pursued an ambivalent relationship with musicians and music. The religion first arrived in North Africa around 640 AD, and though it now thrives mostly in North and West Africa, Islam once stretched as far as the ancient city of Great Zimbabwe,

thousands of miles to the south. Initially, music played no significant role in Islam, but musical expression enriched Koranic chanting and the call to prayer. But the centuries have seen steady growth in Islamic musical traditions—the development of classical styles and compositions and the rise of dignified star singers, beginning with **Ibn Misjah** and **Ziryab**, "The Blackbird," an exiled Iraqi who lived in the Maghreb and later helped originate Moorish Spain's Andalusian music tradition, which influenced Western classic music. Often shunned by orthodox Islam, mystical sects have also developed trance music traditions, where the performance becomes a form of devotion designed to induce states of higher consciousness.

In pre-Islamic North Africa, women dominated the music of the Berbers who lived there. In the past century, women have often ranked as the most celebrated singers in North African traditions. But with noteworthy exceptions, such as the women *iggawin* (traditional musicians) of Mauritania, they typically play instruments only in private settings, not as a profession.

Today, religion and music find themselves increasingly at odds in this region. With both Muslim fundamentalism and frank, youth-oriented pop music on the rise, the confrontation can reach deadly extremes. In Algeria, pop singers and producers face the real possibility of summary death sentences as punishment for openly discussing the passions of youth, romantic love, or drinking alcohol. In Egypt, which has also seen violence in the arts world, every pop song must win the approval of government censors before it hits the market.

Ethiopia and Sudan, technically outside North Africa and not exclusively Islamic, join Egypt and the countries of the Maghreb in this section. Christianity dominates in Ethiopia, though many more ancient cultures survive there as well. In Sudan, Africa's largest country, the Nile flows from animist and Christian areas in the south to the Islamic north, but in contrast to most other northern African nations, history has not yet quelled religious and cultural animosities, and endemic warfare persists between these sharply divided regions. Though the British colonized Egypt and Sudan, the Italians briefly held Libya and Ethiopia, and the Spanish controlled northern Morocco and the Western Sahara, the French controlled more territory, had more widespread influence and left a more European imprint on this region.

Opposite: Fès, Morocco   Left: Chaba Zahouania
Above: Rabat, Morocco

OUM KALSOUM and EGYPT'S CLASSIC SINGERS

An orchestra fills the stage. Violins and cellos slide through languid modes, swelling with woodwinds in the high voices while fat string bass and taut hand drums spell out rhythms from a slow march to a canter. At the center, the great **Oum Kalsoum** guides her robust voice through precise oscillations and dynamics that express depths of emotion, especially the vocal quality called *shaggan*, "grieving." From her 1921 debut until death in 1975, Oum (Mother) Kalsoum's reputation spread throughout the Arabic-speaking world from her base in Cairo. Israeli radio still uses the beloved Oum Kalsoum to woo Palestinian listeners. Born in 1905, Kalsoum used to dress as a boy to sing without harassment from authorities. At the height of her career, politicians took care not to compete with her weekly radio show in which she would unfold lyric poems, taking up to an hour to complete one piece. When Kalsoum died, millions flooded onto the Cairo streets to mourn her. She left no children, just 286 songs, 132 of them based on the poems of Ahmed Ramy. Born in 1907, the most influ-

ential composer and popularizer of Egyptian classical music, **Mohamed Abdel Wahab,** got his start as the pretty voice behind a fading, female star, lip-synching on stage. In the '30s, he helped bring Lebanon's Baidophon label to Cairo. Following the path of composer **Sayed Darweesh,** Abdel Wahab blended classical tradition and modern film music. In 1965, at a time when he had ventured into experiments with popular music and western sounds, he wrote Oum Kalsoum's celebrated "Enta Omri" ("You Are All My Years") her first song with electric guitar. Abdel Wahab died in 1991. A great singer, and like Abdel Wahab, also a film star, **Abd el-Halim Hafez** (1927-77) took to the stage in his twenties, lending his voice to President Abdel Nasser's 1952 nationalist revolution and earning the epithet "Nightingale of the Nile." Working with Wahab though, he went on to extend his light, pop-oriented songs into long form neo-classical works in Oum Kalsoum's distinguished tradition. Years after their deaths, these musicians still outsell all their contemporary competitors.

● *Oum Kalsoum*, **Enta Omri** (Sono, Egypt) • **Amal Hayati** (Sono, Egypt) • **Retrospective** (Artists Arabes Associés, France) • **Hagartek** (EMI, Egypt) • **Fat el Mead** (Sono Cairo, Egypt) ● *Mohammed Abdel Wahab*, **Mohamed Abd el-Wahab, V. I—X** (Clube du Disque Arabe, France) • **V. I, III, IV** of **Les Archives de la Musique Arabe** (Club du Disque Arabe, France) • **Magnoun Leila** (Cairophon, Lebanon) ● *Abd el-Halim Hafez*, **Qariat Al-Fengan** (Soutelphan, Egypt) • **Qululith** (Soutelphan, Egypt) • **Enregistrement Public au Palais des Congrès a Paris, V. 1-2** (live recordings) (Blue Silver, France)

ALI HASSAN KUBAN, MOHAMED MOUNIR and NUBIAN MUSIC

Pharaonic, Roman, Byzantine, Arab, Ethiopian, and East and West African cultures all have echoes in southern Egypt's Nubia region. The "Captain of Nubian Music," **Ali Hassan Kuban,** got his start serenading passengers on boats traveling the

Nile. He also worked week-long Nubian weddings, where complex *tar* (frame drum) and hand-clap rhythms, *girba* (bagpipes) and traditional chants enliven pre-nuptial bashes. After playing in the orchestra for the opera *Aida* in 1949, Ali began to work the clubs in

Cairo, Alexandria and Aswan, revamping the old music with sax, electric guitars, bass, organ, trumpet and accordion. In 1964, the newly built Aswan dam created Lake Nasser, the world's biggest man-made lake. The project displaced 100,000 Nubians many of whom went to cities, filled with a nostalgic love for their buried past. Employing over 60 musicians and operating seven bands, Ali still plays traditional and popular music for both urban and rural Nubian enclaves. Meanwhile, the top singer from a 1970s wave of Nubian migration, **Mohamed Mounir** sings with a powerful, plaintive voice. He presents himself as an Egyptian, intent on reaching beyond the Nubian communities. Mounir came from Aswan and knows Nubian tradition, but he tempers his roots with international pop flavor, and courts the young intellectuals in Cairo's *al jeel* pop scene, addressing broad social and political themes such as the Arab-Israeli conflict.

● *Ali Hassan Kuban*, **From Nubia to Cairo** (Shanachie, US/Piranha, Germany) • **Walk Like a Nubian** (Piranha, Germany) ● *Mohamed Mounir*, **Iftah Aibek** (Sound of America, Egypt) • **Mishwar** (Sound of America, Egypt) • **Mohamed Mounir** (Monsun-Line, Germany) • **Wast el-Daira** (Monsun-Line, Germany)

AHMED ADAWEYAH AND SHAABI STARS

After Egypt's demoralizing defeat by Israel in the 1967 war, new sounds developed in Cairo as young Egyptians sought ways to reaffirm themselves in a fast-paced, changing world. Internationally savvy, high-tech *al jeel* became the music of the educated, well-to-do youth. Meanwhile, in working-class neighborhoods, a brash new sound called *shaabi*, which means "of the people" bloomed into view. Shaabi has old, rural origins, but also refers to a modern urban musical style, often using western and electric instruments. Shaabi musicians popularized short song forms and lyrics dealing with everyday social themes, paralleling the development of "working class" politics. These embers caught fire in Egypt in the '70s, ignited by the onset of affordable cassette technology.

Shamelessly rude and comic in his themes and lyrics, **Ahmed Adaweyah** sparked the shaabi explosion with his first cassette in 1971. The music can evoke sadness and nostalgia, but more often fits tales of survival in the city and working class pride to breathless rhythms and rough-edged musical productions. Ahmed and his followers shocked some listeners and delighted others with unabashed straight talk and new takes on traditional social music. In shaabi, old, folkloric chants slide into rap, while hand-clapping and dancing *oud* melodies ornament slamming, bass-driven dance mixes. Ahmed has had songs on topics from sexual attraction to the Gulf War banned from radio play. He remains popular, although less so since his move to a more programmed electronic sound that old fans find emasculated.

Shaabi stars no longer develop their reputations in the clubs along Pyramid Road, but many work at prviate parties and in Cairo studios. Shaabi singers must master the art of *mawal*, improvised commentary and storytelling used to drive home a song's message. **Shabaan Abdul Raheem** worked as an ironing man until he began recording shaabi hits in his big, rough voice. Spiking his pro-Egypt, anti-foreign sentiments with rap profanity, Shabaan sells well, despite or perhaps aided by the fact that a number of his cassettes have been banned. Though he can sell 100,000 or more of each release, he continues to lead a simple life, tending to his chickens and goats in his old neighborhood. Singers **Sami Ali** and **Sahar Hamdy** take a still bolder rap approach and have earned the radio ban for a number of sexually explicit songs.

In the '90s, young shaabi stars like **Khaled Agag, Hassan el Asmar**, **Magdy Talaat**, and **Magdy Shabin** emphasize the bleeps, pops and whines of synthesizers and drum machines. Outsiders may find the results tacky—to the point of comedy, or perhaps seduction—but techno-shaabi parallels developments in youth pop across North Africa as a large, restless generation of teenagers announces its presence and its openness to new ideas.

⊙ *Ahmed Adaweyah, **Vol. 1** (EMI, Greece)* • **Sineen** (Adaweyat, Egypt)
⊙ *Amr Diab, **Ayamna** (Delta, Egypt)* • **Matkhafish** (Delta, Egypt) • **Wilumuni** (Delta, Egypt)
⊙ *Aida, **Alabali** (Americana, Egypt)* • **Min Zaman** (American, Egypt)
⊙ *Ihab Tawfid, **Murasil** (Slam/Sonar, Egypt)*
⊙ *Various, **Yalla: Hitlist Egypt** (Mango, US)*

Left: Amr Diab   Above: Aida

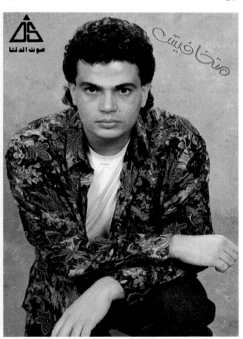

AL JEEL

While *shaabi* rocked Cairo slums in the '70s, the lighter, more polished sound of *al jeel* developed as an Egyptian alternative to foreign pop. Spitting in the eye of reverent, old-school classicism, producers programmed synthesizers to play quarter-tone scales and sought out lyricists who could spin a romantic yarn, and singers who could both charm with sweet voices and look cute on cassette jackets. People called the music al jeel—"the new wave"—emphasizing its new spin on Nubian, Bedouin and Egyptian roots. Seminal al jeel producer **Hameed Sharay** came from Libya in the wake

of Qadhafi's 1974 crackdown on foreign culture. In Cairo, Hameed developed stars like **Hanan** and **Ehab**. Classically trained, and a rare woman in al jeel, Hanan's shrill, wild voice bursts with exuberance—they call her "Egypt's smile." Al jeel's simplification of scales, vocal nuances, and texts left highbrow radio programmers cold. But the predominant, under-25 crowd, embraced the sound as their own. Handsome **Amr Dieb** topped the scene in the late '80s, breaking traditionally sedate stage conventions to romp and jump around for crowds of 50,000 or more. Other new artists include *shaabi* defector **Abdel el Musree** and his group **Salamat**, who produced a whimsical Nubian al jeel release *Mambo El Soudani* in 1994. Feeling that

al jeel had lapsed into stale imitation by the mid-'80s, multi-faceted producer and composer **Fathy Salama** broke from the scene to play more rocking, dry-eyed pop with his band **Sharkiat**. One of the newest on the scene, Alexandria's **Mustafa Amar** has become a top-selling teen heart-throb.

⊙ *Various, **Yalla: Hitlist Egypt** (Mango, US)*
⊙ *Hussain el Masry, **Ra'etak** (Erde, Germany)*
⊙ *Sharkiat (w/Fathy Salama), **Camel Dance** (Face Music, Switzerland)*
⊙ *Salamat, **Mambo el Soudani: Nubian Al Jeel Music from Cairo** (Piranha, Germany)*
⊙ *Salamat & Les Musiciens du Nil, **Salam Delta** (Piranha, Germany)*

CHEIKHA REMITTI AND THE PIONEERS OF RAI

The rebellious pop style called *rai*, meaning "opinion," has dominated Algeria's youth market since the '70s. Rai has origins in Bedouin oral traditions, in the music of Berbers who moved from the Algerian mountains to the cities of Oran and Algiers, and in Andalusian music that came to North African ports after the Moors were thrown out of Spain in 1492. By the 1930s, these elements had coalesced in a style called *wahrani* championed by *cheikhas*—female singers—in the bars of Algeria's "Little Paris," the coastal city of Oran. Cheikhas voiced the complaints of working class people in French colonial Algeria, upsetting officials. They also sang openly about sex, upsetting conservative *mujahedin* rebels. Just the same, with her husky voice and inviting sexuality, **Cheikha Remitti El Ghizania** seduced a mass following beginning with her 1936 debut recording. When revolution stirred in the '50s, Remitti and others, then known as *shaabi* musicians, backed the cause. Trumpeter **Bellemou Messaoud** made a career of accompanying the first *pop rai* singers in the early '60s, around the time of independence. Schooled in Spanish music, Bellemou replaced wahrani's *qasbah* flute with trumpet or sax, and customized a quarter-tone accordion. Working with singer **Belkacem Bouteldja**, he stole the spotlight from a furious Remitti. Soon however, the new government interfered, banning concerts and liquor sales in 1967, and limiting rai music to private weddings and the commercial cassette market. In this climate, the late producer **Rachid Baba Ahmed**, a fan of rock, soul, and funk, set up a basic eight-track studio and became pop rai's number one hitmaker, producing blockbuster releases that launched legendary rai careers for artists like **Khaled, Zahouania** and **Fadela**. Today, though over 70 years old, Remitti continues to record.

⊙ Cheikha Remitti, **Rai Roots** (CMM/Buda Musique, France) • **Qhir El Baroud** (Sonodisc, France) • **Sidi Mansour** (*Absolute Records, France*)
⊙ Bellemou Messaoud, **La Père du Rai** (World Circuit, UK)

Left: Cheikha Remitti
Below: Bellemou Messaoud

KHALED, THE KING OF RAI

The terms *cheb* and *chebba*—young man and young woman—put an informal spin on the more dignified musical honorifics *cheikh* and *cheikha* of *wahrani* music. Algeria's bold '70s *rai* singers dispensed with decorum and sang songs that proved shockingly outspoken for Algerians. "Before rai there was poetry," says **Khaled**, still the King of Rai though no longer a cheb. "In wahrani, we didn't talk about chicks or drinking alcohol. To describe love, we talked about a pigeon. I say things directly—I drink alcohol; I love a woman; I am suffering." Born the son of a policeman in Oran around 1960, **Khaled Hadj Brahim** quickly embraced music, singing as a boy at weddings and recording his first single at just 16. By the early '80s, Cheb Khaled hits like "Hada Raykoum" ("So That is What You Desire") alarmed Islamic conservatives with erotic, funky trance rhythms and straight-up lyrics like, "Hey, Mama, your daughter wants me." After his knockout performance at Algeria's first rai festival in 1985, Khaled moved to France, where he recorded *Kutche* with keyboard man **Safi Boutella** and Paris producer Martin Messonier. The record charted a course for the tasteful, punchy international sound

Khaled has since developed with Los Angeles producer Don Was. Working around short, repeating vocal phrases, Khaled blasts out clear, sustained, vibratoless salvos that glide over his beefy dance mixes. Khaled recently had a hit in India, sung in Hindi, and has now begun to reach an American audience, leading the way for other international rai artists, notably the younger **Cheb Mami,** who also recorded his last two records in L.A.. Crossover rai appeals especially to the second generation north Africans, living in France and no longer impressed by cheaply produced Algerian cassettes. A potential target for Algerian Islamic militants, Khaled now lives permanently in France.

◉ Khaled, **The Best of Cheb Khaled** (Blue Silver, France) • **Hada Raykoum** (Triple Earth/Stern's, UK) • **Khaled** (Barclay, France) • **N'ssi N'ssi** (Mango, US) • **El Marsem** (Editions Bouarfa, France) • **Serbi Serbi** (Editions Bouarfa, France) • **Le Bab** (Editions Hassania, Morocco)
◉ Cheb Khaled & Safy Boutella, **Kutché** (Stern's, US)
◉ Cheb Mami, **Let Me Rai** (Rhythm Safari/Priority, US) • **Saida** (Blue Silver, France) • **Le Prince du Rai** (Editions Bouarfa, France)

ZAHOUANIA, FADELA AND SAHRAOUI

Since its dramatic rise in the '70s, Algerian *pop rai* has produced a long line of seductive *chebs* and sassy *chebbas*. One of the first, **Chebba Fadela** set her sights on the stage from girlhood. After hearing her warm, blossoming voice at wedding performances, audiences dubbed her "la petite Remitti." Like **Khaled**, Fadela then worked with producer **Rachid Ahmed** to record landmark hits, notably her '79 smash, "Ana Ma H'lali Ennoum" ("Sleep Doesn't Matter to me Anymore"). She married singer **Cheb Sahraoui** in '82, and they've performed together ever since and recorded two international records for Mango, *N'Sel Fik* (*You Are Mine*) and *Hana Hana*. Sahraoui, who trained at an Oran conservatory, favors a keyboard-heavy sound for the couple's act these days. The band also uses rhythm guitar, bass, drums, and the sharp-toned, goblet-shaped hand drum called *derbouka*. Songs often begin with an arrhythmic vocal preamble and then kick in, *derbouka* and vocal pushing ahead while the drums pull back with syncopated, backbeat accents coaxing dancers into character-

istic undulations, their arms extended gracefully skyward. Born **Halima Mazzi** in 1959, another enduring pop rai star, **Zahouania** sang in semi-classical orchestras at 13 and produced her first rai cassette in 1980. Ten years later, she became one of the lucky few rai singers to reach an international audience with her Mango release *Nights Without Sleeping.*

◉ Zahouania, **Nights Without Sleeping** (Mango, US) • **Lalla Mahlak ou Maglak** (Gafaiti Production, France) • **La Reine du Rai** (Blue Silver, France) • **Sidi Belkacem** (Editions Hassania, Morocco)
◉ Chaba Fadela & Cheb Sahraoui, **You Are Mine** (Mango, US) • **Hana Hana** (Mango, US) • **In New York—Feel My Hurt** (Aladin le Musicien, France) • **Cheb Sahraoui & Chaba Fadela** (Celluloid, France)
◉ Various, **Rai Rebels** (Stern's Earthworks) • **Pop Rai and Rachid Style** (Stern's Earthworks)

Left: Chebba Fadela

HASNI, NASRO AND THE CRISIS OF RAI

Algeria's political instability puts growing pressure on *rai* music. Cassette producers still crank out releases—mostly name singers backed by programmed keyboards and drum machines—causing some to complain of "too many titles by too few names." 1990's stars **Cheb Nasro** and **Cheb Hasni** have sought to avoid conflicts with Islamic extremists by singing romantic, lovers rai, after the controversies of the late '80s. Born in '68 in Gamvetta district of Oran to a welder's

family, Hasni sang at weddings and then recorded with **Zahouania**. His break came in '87 when he covered the risqué "El Berraka" ("We Made Love in a Cemetery"). During the government's 1990-92 ban on concerts, Hasni recorded extensively, bringing his total to over 80 cassettes in six years, and selling up to 400,000 copies of each. Hasni's international release *Rai Love* reveals strong pop instincts and a big voice, smoother than Khaled's, but also powerful. Hasni was fatally shot in front of his house in November 1994 after receiving written death threats from Islamic extremists. Gunmen also targeted rai's top producer, **Rachid Baba Ahmed**, shot dead on the street in Oran in February, 1995, during the holy month of Ramadan. Though the true stories behind these killings remain elusive, they underscore rai's uncertain future in a country deeply divided about governance and morality, where pop singers and Islamic forces woo the same disaffected working class constituency.

Though rai gets the most attention internationally, Algeria also has a roots music scene that includes Kabylie Berber singers performing mostly acoustic music. **Houria Aichi**, with her *shawiya* style, sings accompanied prominently by *bendir* drums playing delicate, spatial

rhythms from as far south as the Hoggar Mountains in the Algerian Sahara. Internationally renowned Berber singer **Djur Djura** showed star talent from an early age, but her fiercely conservative family objected so strenuously to her career that they have since mounted life-threatening physical attacks on the singer. For all her success, Djur has paid a high price for living as a free woman. Through her music, her writing and film documentaries, Djur champions the condition of Algerian women, and also the nation's neglected educational system. Another talented Berber singer, **Matoub Lounes**, lives and records in Paris.

❍ Hasni, **Rani Mourak** (Gafaiti Production, France) • **Rai Love** (Buda, France) • **The Best of...** (Blue Silver, France)
❍ Cheb Nasro, **The Best of...** (Blue Silver, France) • **El Hammam** (Blue Moon Productions/Mélodie, France)
❍ Djur Djura, **Adventures in Afropea, v. 2** (Luaka Bop, US)
❍ Idir, **Les Chasseurs de Lumiere** (Blue Silver, France)
❍ Matoub Lounes, **Thissirth N'Endama** (Blue Silver, France)
❍ Houria Aichi, **Hawa** (Tempo/Auvidis, France)
❍ Thissas, **Chant et Musique de Kabylie** (Blue Silver, France)
❍ Ouardia, **Assirem** (Editions Oubuya Rachid, France)
❍ Various, **Folklore Kabylie** (Club du Disque Arabe, France)

Left: Hasni   Below: Mustapha Baqbou

MOROCCO'S '70S ROOTS REVIVAL
AND NEW FUSIONS

Moroccan cities have long supported *shaabi*, "popular" groups playing in cafés and recording cassettes for the local market. Traditionally, shaabi songs begin with slow, explorative introductions and move towards a fast ending section called *leseb*. Shaabi founders from the '50s and '60s, **Abdelwahab Doukali** and **Hamid Zahir,** remain the most popular names. But during the '70s, a second wave of shaabi groups slowed the pace and sharpened the sound, inspired as much by Indian music and the Beatles as by the prevalent Egyptian pop they competed with directly.

Three groups, **Nass El-Ghiwane, Jil Jilala** and **Lem Chaheb,** spearheaded the '70s rise of shaabi. Nass El-Ghiwane, which means "People of the Street," began as an avant-garde political theater group in Marrakesh in the '60s. Following the imprisonment of the group, the murder of one member and suicide of another, and exile to France, Nass El-Ghiwane returned as a five-piece roots-fusion band singing hypnotic, message-laden

trance songs. Lead singer **Boujmia** criticized the powerful and sang about the trials of the poor. Since his death in a car crash in the '80s, the remaining quartet has continued with a strong flavor of the Arab-African *Gnawa* music in their sound. Jil Jilala started out in 1972, also as a theater troupe. The group's music draws from the orchestral *malhoun* tradition, where lengthy musical compositions accompany classical poetry. Jil Jilala now uses Gnawa rhythms and the double-reed *ghaita*, as well as fretless *bouzouki* and two *bendirs* (frame drums) to bolster the beat. The third crucial shaabi group, the five-piece Lem Chaheb, has ventured furthest into western idioms, pushing the boundaries of a music scene wary of foreign influences. Guitar and bouzouki ace **Lamrani Moulay Cherif**, the group's star attraction, plays over traditional percussion, electric bass, horns, voices, and now, inevitably, drum machines. In 1985, Lem Chaheb toured with the German fusion band Dissidenten and played on their record *Sahara Electric*. Continuing the roots pop tradition in the

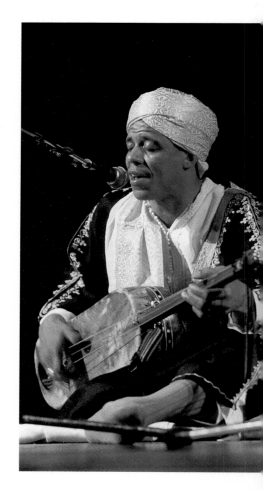

'80s, a young group **Muluk el Hwa** plays all acoustic music incorporating Gnawa material. Their recent cassette *Casbah* sold over 200,000 copies in Spain.

Meanwhile, Morocco now hosts its own active *rai* scene. In contrast to the roots groups, rai singers like **Bouchra, Cheb Achab** and **Bouchebcheb** gleefully embrace modernity—cheesy keyboards, grunge guitar, reggae organ, sizzling drum machines, and often disco's pumping beat. Still further out on the pop curve, a new generation of Moroccan youth experiments with techno-aesthetics, jungle loops and rap shock value, while still guarding elements of tradition. Any mention of the troublesome female spirit Aisha Kandisha alarms elders. Out to shock, **Aisha**

Kandisha's Jarring Effects formed in '87 and has now joined the ranks of Moroccan musicians to work with producer Bill Laswell.

Since moving to Belgium in the late '60s, the gifted, blind musician **Hassan Erraji** has charted new territory for Moroccan traditional music. His group **Arabesque**'s 1989 debut edges the frenetic, expressive twang of oud melodies towards flamenco fire in a cool, jazz-rock setting. In two subsequent albums, Hassan plays violin, *qanoon* zither, *nay* flute and the double-reed *ghaita*.

⦿ Nass El-Ghiwane, **The Best of…** (Blue Silver, France) • **Chants Gnawa du Moroc** (Buda, France) • **Chants d'Espoir** (Hillali, France) • **Wannadi Ana** (Kan, France) • **Jil Jilala, Chamaa** (Kan Cleopatre, France) • **El Chamaa** (Kan, Morocco)

⦿ Mustapha Baqbou, **Mustafa Baqbou** (World Circuit, UK)

⦿ Lem Chaheb, **La Chanson Populaire Morocaine** (Artists Arabe Associés, France) • **El Arab** (Editions Hassania, France) • **Lemchaheb (El Jounoud)** (Hassania, Morocco)

⦿ Aisha Kandisha's Jarring Effects, **El Buya** (Barbarity, Switzerland) • **Shabeesation** (Barbarity, Switzerland)

⦿ Hassan Erraji & Arabesque, **Nikriz** (Riverboat, UK)

⦿ Dissidenten, **Life at the Pyramids** (Shanachie, US) • **Sahara Elektrik** (Shanachie, US)

⦿ Hamed Zahir (oud), **El Al Hubur wa El Shehem** (Editions Hassania, Morocco)

⦿ Rabih Abou Khalil, **The Sultan's Picnic** (Enja)

⦿ Nouamane, **Jebel al Atlas** (Adouaa Al Madina, France)

⦿ Various (rai), **Oujda-Casablanca Introspections, v. 1** (Barbarity, Switzerland) • **Trance 2** (Ellipsis Arts, US)

THE LURE OF JAJOUKA AND THE ATLAS MOUNTAIN BERBERS

The trance music of the Moroccan village of Jajouka in the foothills of the Atlas mountains has lured many westerners. Legend holds that descendants of Berbers took in the last members of a 7th century Iraqi army, who were found playing beautiful songs near the village. These survivors founded Jajouka's famed musical clan. The celebrated author and composer Paul Bowles has written about the village's annual reenactment of the ancient Rites of Pan, performed through eight ecstatic, moonlit nights to ensure fertility and maintain balance between the sexes. The wailing, oboe-like, double-reed *ghaitas*, and the thundering *tebel* drums accompany this ritual. Beat poet William Burroughs once called the **Master Musicians of Jajouka** a "4,000 year old rock-and-roll band," and following that cue, the Rolling Stones' Brian Jones made a psychedelic record with the group in the '70s. Jazz colossus Ornette Coleman also recorded with musicians in Jajouka. More recently, New York producer and bassist Bill Laswell made a definitive field recording of the group, as well as a crossover release by multi-instrumentalist **Bachir Attar**, who became Jajouka's *maalim* or master when his father died in the late '80s.

Berber speakers live throughout North Africa. For centuries, neither Islamic nor French invaders could penetrate their strongholds in the high valleys of the Atlas Mountains, where they preserved their non-Arab language, and their ritual and recreational music. Born in 1960 in Khemisset, **Najat Aatabou** might have lived out her days singing at family ceremonies had she not been discovered by a Casablanca talent scout in 1983. But when her debut cassette "J'en ai Marre" ("I'm Sick of It") sold nearly

500,000 copies, her obscurity ended. Recording both with orchestral backing and the spare staccato rhythms of the *bendir* frame drum and plucked-string, percussive *lotar*, Najat has evolved her songs of heartbreak and loneliness into humorous, frank tales of urban romance.

Above: Bachir Attar

⦿ Master Musicians of Jajouka featuring Bachir Attar, **Apocalypse Across the Sky** (Axiom/Mango, US)

⦿ Bachir Attar, **The Next Dream** (CMP Records, Germany)

⦿ Najat Aatabou, **The Voice of the Atlas** (GlobeStyle, UK) • **The Best of Najat Aatabou** (Blue Silver, France) • **Goul El Hak El Mout Kayna** (MK7, France) • **Nouveau '92** (Editions Hassania, Morocco)

⦿ Various, **Morocco: Crossroads of Time** (Ellipsis Arts, US)

"Y ou'll find that Gnawis live all over the world," says **Abdenbi Binizi**, a musician from Morocco's musically gifted Islamic brotherhood. Not a people as such, Gnawa trace their ancestries to various parts of sub-Saharan Africa, and claim as their patron saint Sidi Bilal, the Prophet Mohammed's first *muezzin*, or caller to prayer. Morocco captured the Malian city of Timbuktu in the 16th century, and brought Bambara-speaking slaves across the Sahara. The fact that the Gnawa's main string instrument—the *sintir* or *gimbri*—resembles a large version of the Bambara *ngoni*, suggests that many of the Gnawa came from there. Today, Gnawa gather to play music and dance acrobatically in Marrakesh's traditional square, Jemaa el Fna, once a crossroads for caravans from Mali, Mauritania and points south. Gnawa play deeply hypnotic trance music, marked by low-toned, rhythmic sintir melodies, call-and-response singing, hand clapping and

THE GNAWA BROTHERHOOD

cymbals called *qaraqish*. Gnawa *dardeba* ceremonies use music and dance to evoke ancestral saints who can drive out evil, cure psychological ills, or remedy scorpion stings. The album *Night Spirit Masters*, produced by Bill Laswell and Richard Horowitz in 1990, provides an evocative studio experience with a variety of Gnawa musicians, including sintir player/vocalists **Mustapha Baqbou** (from **Jil Jilala**) and **Abdelqader Oughassal**. One young Gnawa, **Hassan Hakmoun**, has settled in New York where he combines traditional instruments, keyboards and guitars to create a fusion that nods to Hendrix, even as the rhythm section moves back and forth between Jemaa el Fna and the Lower East Side. American jazz musicians, notably Randy Weston and Pharoah Sanders, have also worked

with Gnawa to find an intersection between jazz exploration and *dardeba* trance.

- Amida Boussou, **Gnawa Leila** (Al Sur, France)
- Various, **Gnawa Music of Marrakesh: Night Spirit Masters** (Axiom/Mango, US)
- Gnawa Halwa, **Rhabaouine** (Blanca Li Records/Mélodie, France)
- Maleem Mahmoud Ghania w/Pharoah Sanders, **The Trance of Seven Colors** (Axiom/Island, US)
- Hassan Hakmoun & Zahar, **Trance** (RealWorld, UK)
- Various, **Moroccan Trance Music: Jilala & Gnawa** (Sub Rosa Records, France)
- Various (Gnawa and Berber), **Hafla!** (Radiant Future, UK)

Above: Hassan Hakmoun   Left: Gnawis Samir Zhougari, Hassan Zhougari, Abdenbi Binizi, Azziz Rad

ROOTS OF ETHIOPIAN POP

E thiopia has known much isolation since its rise from the dust of the Axum kingdom in 500 BC. Already a Christian land when Islam swept through northern Africa, Ethiopia survived a bout with Portuguese colonialism only to descend into civil wars after forcing the conquerors out in the 19th century. The Emperor Haile Selassie came to the throne in 1930, intending to modernize the country. Though his rule survived World War II-era domination by Italy, it ended in failure in 1974, when the repressive, "Marxist" Mengistu regime once again cut Ethiopia off—especially from the west—until 1991. This history of suffering finds expression in *achinoy*, a melancholy quality treasured in

Ethiopian music. Though the country hosts 75 ethnic groups, the Amharic-speaking people from the central highlands around Addis Ababa have mostly dominated popular music. Since ancient times, Amharic *azmari* musicians have recited oral histories accompanied by the *krar* (lyre), *masenqo* (one-string fiddle), and *washint* (flute). In the '20s, the young Selassie brought in Armenian refugees from Jerusalem to form the **Bodyguard Orchestra**, and well into the '70s, similar military brass bands accompanied the nation's early recording artists—the poetic **Tilahoun Gessesse**, his successful protégé the "Hindi-styled" **Neway Debebe**, and the ultimate best seller, **Mahmoud Ahmed**. From the start, these pio-

neers diversified, singing both traditional and popular repertoires, working with a variety of bands, and playing the grand halls as well as the *tedjbets* or beer halls of Addis, where dancers shake shoulders, heave chests and snap their heads back in the customary *iskista* dance. Fashioning a unique, sensuous pop tradition, these singers honor the old *tchik-tchik-ka* rhythm—a fast, lopsided triplet beat—but arrange their smooth, quivering voices in call-and-response with trumpets and saxophones, and hike the music's emotional pitch to rock-and-roll levels.

- Mahmoud Ahmed, **Ere Mela Mela** (Hannibal/Rykodisc, US)
- Neway Debebe, **Neway Debebe, V. 1-3** (Tango Music, US)
- Tilahun Gessesse, **Tilahun Gessesse, v. 1-2** (Ethio Grooves, US)

MAURITANIA'S DIMI MINT ABBA

The vast desert nation of Mauritania lies between Morocco and Senegal. Over the years, drought has concentrated three quarters of its once-nomadic people in cities. The coastal capital, Nouakchott has gone from 20,000 to half a million in just 35 years. Descended from Bedouin conquerors and Berber refugees from Morocco, modern Moors include both Bidan, who claim ancestry from Bedouins and Berbers, and Haratin, who descend from Arab-speaking, liberated slaves. The country's strict caste system puts musicians, *iggawin*, at the bottom. Nevertheless, musicians must undertake elaborate study, men on the four-stringed, hourglass-shaped *tidinit* lute, and women on the 10- to 14-string harp lute, the *ardin*. Players can learn three "ways" to play, the white, the black, and the spotted, and within each "way," there are five modes each corresponding to a life phase or emotion—*karr, fagu, lakhal, labyad* and *lebtayt*. Born in 1958 to a musical family **Dimi Mint Abba** has enjoyed top billing in Mauritanian music since she won the International Oum Kalsoum Song Contest in Tunisia in 1977. Her winning song "Sawt Elfan" ("Art's Plume") argues that artists play a more important role than warriors in society. Dimi has one international release recorded in England in 1990 with husband **Khalifa Ould Eide** on guitar, vocals and tidinit, and his two daughters on percussion. Backed by tambourine, hand claps, and one deep, dry-sounding kettledrum (*tabola*), Dimi and Khalifa pluck and jangle their lutes and exchange vocal leads, telling stories as they shift among related musical modes. Catchy melodies and extended improvisation grace this severe, but beguiling music.

⊙ *Khalifa Ould Eide & Dimi Mint Abba,* **Moorish Music from Mauritania** (*World Circuit, UK*)

⊙ *Ensemble el Moukhadrami,* **Musiques et Chants Traditionnels de Mauritanie** (*Institut du Monde Arabe/Blue Silver, France*)

THE '70S AND '80S: CURFEW IN ETHIOPIA

Tilahoun Gessesse unleashes his powerful, snaking voice over a loping, horn-driven groove, ornamented by the plucked rhythms of the *krar*. The slinky feel suggests a Latin tinge and a taste of soul. Dark pentatonic scales, unfamiliar even in the palette of North African music, convey desire, remorse and forbidding. When Mengistu came to power in 1974, a 10 p.m. curfew drove musicians into studios, where session bands like **Roha Band**, **Wallias Band** and later **Ethio Stars** developed. Producer and talent scout **Ali Tango** exploited the dawn of cassettes in 1978 to boost typical sales from 3000 LPs in the old days, to as many as 100,000 tapes. Private parties lasted

until five a.m., when the curfew ended. Despite these constraining circumstances, some 50 male and female singers maintained recording careers. **Mahmoud Ahmed**, who started out as a shoeshine boy in Addis, emerged as a top star, fitting his highly melodic approach both with the old-fashioned **Imperial Bodyguard Band**, and the up-and-coming **Roha Band,** which, with over 250 releases to its credit, has now dominated Ethiopia's pop scene for over a decade. Singing with **Yohannes Tekola's Wallias Band,** the soulful **Alemayehu Eshete** evoked James Brown and Little Richard. Also with the Wallias Nand, **Netsanet Mellesse** applied her sweet, choirgirl voice to suggestive, electric pop.

The era's third great backing band **Ethio Stars** formed in '81, bringing in rock and reggae, but staying loyal to the old pentatonic scales and the *tchik-tchik-ka* rhythm, essential to the Ethiopian sound.

• *Roha Band,* **Roha Band Tour** (*Aman International, US*)
• *Tukul Band & Ethio Stars,* **Amharic Hits** (*Piranha, Germany*)
• *Alamayehu Eshete,* **Addis Ababa** (*Shanachie, US*)
• *Netsanet Mellesse,* **Spirit of Sheba** (*Shanachie, US*) (*also titled* **Dodge** *distributed by Stern's, UK*)
• *Various,* **Ethiopian Groove: The Golden Seventies** (*Blue Silver, France*)

ASTER AWEKE

In Ethiopia's poetic tradition called *sam-ennawarq* (wax and gold), one can sing about a cruel lover as a way of mocking the government. During the '80s though, even veiled expressions carried risks, and for this among other reasons, musicians who could often did flee the Mengistu regime to exile in Sudan or the US. Born in Begemdr in the late '50s, **Aster Aweke** began singing professionally in 1977. At the time, female vocalists mostly stood demurely on stage and delivered delicate, breathy tones. But having heard Aretha Franklin, Aster wanted to belt. She quickly tired of the notoriety she earned by following her wilder instincts at home and so moved to Washington, DC in 1979. Singing in restaurants with other expatriate musicians, she built a reputation and soon became the darling of Ethiopian communities in US cities coast-to-coast. Aster's music delivers a strong shot of jazz and pumps out funky dance beats blending horns, keyboards, guitars and drums. Her amazingly agile voice hits with r&b power, but its sweet tone and limber acrobatics suggest a girlish delicacy and vulnerability. Aster's 1989 international debut, *Aster*, awakened a growing world music audience to Ethiopian music. Though she now moves back and forth between the US and Europe, Aster's original and adventurous work has always found a receptive audience back home in Ethiopia.

🔘 Aster Aweke, *Aster Aweke* (Triple Earth, UK) • *Kabu* (Columbia, US)

ETHIOPIA TODAY

Much has changed since the Mengistu regime fell in 1991. Finally able to travel, established stars tour frequently to play for exiled communities long denied direct contact with their favorite singers. Meanwhile in Addis, a new generation, eager to jettison reminders of a depressing past, turn their ears to Kenyan pop, and to American rap and reggae. A star while still in his teens, **Hebiste Tiruneh** heads up a new stable of pop singers that now also includes **Yihuneh Belaye, Chache Tadesse,** and **Hamelmal Abate,** the country's top female singer at present. The **Abyssinia Band,** led by **Davit Kassa** grew popular, even though it radically altered the sound of local music by introducing the seven-note western scale. Though now defunct, Abyssinia's inventive arrangements pioneered the use of international pop formulas previously off-limits, like Zairean *soukous* guitar. Keyboard player and arranger **Abegassu Kibrework Shiota** has worked with stars **Aster Aweke** and **Tilihoun Gessesse.** Now working and studying in the US, Abegassu plays in the **Admas Band.**

Perhaps the biggest change in Ethiopian music is that long-dominant Amharic music now competes with neo-traditional styles from regions like Tigray, Gonder and Oromo. Tigrayan **Kiross Alemayehu** spent four years in Mengistu's prisons for his songs about democracy accompanied by hand clapping, *krar,* and *masenqo.* Now he and fellow Tigrayan musician **Zerihun Wedaho** enjoy freedom and celebrity. The fast, rootsy *gurague* style has produced at least two modern stars, **Mohammed Awel** and **Wabi Abdrehman.** As a group like the **Tukul Band** plays successful pop on electrified traditional instruments—*krar, masenqo* and *washint*—the more mainstream Abyssinia Band responds by using "camel-walk" rhythms in their pop constructions. This newly invigorated environment suggests that the best of Ethiopian pop may lie ahead.

🔘 Tukul Band & Ethio Stars, *Amharic Hits* (Piranha, Germany)
🔘 Abyssinia Band and others, *Music from Ethiopia* (Caprice, US)

SUDAN

After the coming of Islam in the seventh century, present day Sudan thrived by controlling the Nile's trade route to Mecca. Egypt and Britain vied for the region's access to the sea until Lord Kitchener ousted the Islamic Mahdist regime in 1898. England then ruled until Sudan's independence in 1956. A long period of civil war between Muslim north and Christian elements in the south yielded the government of Strongman Colonel Nimeiri in 1969. Nimeiri tried to impose Islamic law, *sharia*, in 1983, but instead fell in a coup two years later. Since then, Sudan has endured two military regimes, civil war and famine.

Before independence, **Ibrahim al-Kashif** became the first Sudanese pop singer, backed by a full Egyptian-style orchestra. **Ahmad al-Mustafa** sang modernized folk songs, popular in '50s, but his glory days came when he penned "Ristair Sudan" the Nimeiri regime's anthem. The northern capital Khartoum developed a good live music scene, as well as television and radio, though not a recording industry. Since its start in 1969, Khartoum's Institute for Music and Drama has produced much impressive talent, including Sudan's three most popular singers, **Abdel Aziz El Mubarak, Abdel Gadir Salim** and **Muhamed Gubara.**

The most successful of these, **Abdel Aziz El Mubarak** started in the '70s. He came from Wad Medani, a village of musicians, but made his name singing urban love tales, backed by his ten-piece, accordion-led band. Abdel Aziz

played at a WOMAD festival in England in 1988 and subsequently recorded international releases. His gentle, reedy voice glides through the band's semi-orchestral textures, with electric guitar and bass adding gravity and ardor. But when improvisers like saxophonist **Hamid Osman Abdalla** and violinist **Mohmdiya** cut loose, the music moves into riveting overdrive. At one time a singer in Abdel Aziz's group, **Abdel Gadir Salim** now also plays *oud* and heads his own group accompanied by tabla and accordion. Singing folk tales using the quarter-tones of the Arab *maqam* scales, Salim champions the rural *merdoum* folklore of his western Sudan home. Though not a controversial singer, Abdel was attacked in the Omdurman Musicians Club outside Khartoum in late 1994 by a religious fanatic intent on killing another singer. Abdel has survived stab wounds to his chest and hand.

Despite stylistic differences, Mubarak and Salim both enjoy rare freedom in Sudan today because they carefully avoid even a whiff of political commentary or indecency in their music. Since the rise of the National Islamic Front in 1989, many other Sudanese musicians have been forced into silence or exile in an environment where mixed dancing is forbidden and love songs get banned on radio if they mention intoxication. Tagged as a "communist," singer **Mohamed Wardi**, one of the few northern artists to win an audience in the Sudanese south as well, fled to Cairo. His band, exiled in Canada, recently recorded a mocking anti-government song with the singer **Hadi**, following in the protest tradition of **Mustafa Sidahmed** and **Yusuf al-Mousli**.

Sudan's most famous musical exile, oud

virtuoso **Hamza el Din**, popularized the Arabic lute in his native Nubia, and went on to study first at the Arab Institute of Music in Cairo, and then in Rome before moving to the US. A composer and ethnomusicologist, Hamza played at the Newport Folk Fest in 1964 and Woodstock in '69. He has worked with artists as diverse as Grateful Dead drummer Mickey Hart and the Kronos Quartet. In Hamza's recent "Nubian Suite," oud encounters *wadaiko* and *shakuhachi*, instruments of the country he now calls home, Japan.

⦿ Abdel Aziz El Mubarak, **Abdel Aziz El Mubarak** (GlobeStyle, UK) • **Straight from the Heart** (World Circuit, UK)

⦿ Abdel Gadir Salim, **Nujum al-Lail / Stars of the Night** (GlobeStyle, UK) • **The Merdoum Kings Play Songs of Love** (World Circuit, UK)

⦿ Abdel Gadir Salim, Abdel Aziz el Mubarak, Mohamed Gubara, **Sounds of Sudan** (World Circuit, UK)

⦿ Mohamed Wardi, **Live in Addis Ababa** (Rags Music, UK)

⦿ Hamza el-Din, **Eclipse** (Rykodisc, US) • **Waterwheel • Songs of the Nile** (JVC, Japan)

⦿ Various, **Sounds of Sudan** (Rounder, US)

Left: Hamza el Din   Above: Abdel Aziz El Mubarak

AFRICAN CROSSOVER DREAMS

Given the web of historical and cultural connections that tie Africa to the world's greatest pop genres—jazz, rock, soul, blues, disco, salsa, merengue, reggae, rap—it's no surprise that musicians all over the world want to collaborate with today's great African maestros. And given the underdeveloped music industries in most African countries, it's also no surprise that world-class African stars want the opportunities and experience such projects offer. Mali's **Salif Keita**, who won a Grammy nomination for *Amen*, his 1992 collaboration with jazz fusion king **Joe Zawinul**, summed the situation up for the New York Times with characteristic dry-eyed clarity, and just a dash of cynicism, "White people who collaborate with African musicians want the inspiration. It's not bad. They get the inspiration and we get popularity."

No doubt the exchange involves risks. The west's drive to find another developing world artist who can rivet international attention as Bob Marley did has at times led artists to distort their music in ways that alienate their home audience and also fail to interest more than a few outsiders. Zimbabwe's **Bhundu Boys** sang in English and flopped. **Youssou N'Dour's** first attempt at progressive rock aesthetics and pop song forms, *The Lion*, proved a commercial disappointment. To his credit, though, Youssou stuck to his plan, and his

1994 single with British/American singer **Neneh Cherry**, "7 Seconds," surprised many by topping European charts and winning MTV Europe's Best Song award. Similarly unexpected, **Deep Forest**, a slick pop packaging of central African Pygmy polyphony, turned into a dancefloor hit and a video sensation in 1993.

Collaborations between stars of different countries typically involve a balance of commercial calculation and musical adventurism. Just the same, the outcomes rarely match expectations. In 1984, when **Paul Simon** headed to South Africa to record with artists virtually unknown in the west, who could have foreseen that they would all share a Grammy award for *Graceland* in 1986? His own career in a rut, Paul wanted to refresh and enhance his creative process. The opening that *Graceland* gave to South African artists like **Ray Phiri** and **Ladysmith Black Mambazo** was the happy by-product of fortuitous timing and South African music's innate appeal, not of a grand marketing scheme.

THE RISE OF WORLD MUSIC

Peter Gabriel also collaborated successfully with African artists, notably when he sang with Youssou N'Dour in 1987, and when he made his worldly film soundtrack for *The Last Temptation of Christ*, released in 1989 as *Passion*. But in contrast to Paul Simon, Peter has made it his primary mission to alert international audiences to the work of world musicians.

Starting in the early '80s, Peter invested much time and money in launching WOMAD (World of Music Arts and Dance), an annual festival of global culture. Peter's RealWorld studio has hosted, among many cross-cultural sessions, an encounter between **Remmy Ongala**'s Tanzanian dance band and American gospel's the **Holmes Brothers**. RealWorld takes some criticism for "Peter Gabriel-izing" African and other sounds, but like WOMAD, RealWorld provides an ongoing workshop for musical dialogue. Its continuity as an institution may count for more than any of its actual releases to date.

Three California-based guitarists have followed their love of African music to serendipitous encounters. Maverick **Henry Kaiser** and all around string master **David Lindley** went to Madagascar in 1991 to record and collaborate with a selection of brilliant musicians from around that huge island nation. On two volumes of *A World Out of Time*, Henry and David skillfully, and for the most part unobtrusively, blend into the Malagasy milieu. In 1993, blues and rock aficionado **Ry Cooder** realized a long-held dream by completing an intimate session with northern Mali's roots guitarist and singer, **Ali Farka Toure**. The result, *Talking Timbuktu*, won a Grammy award in 1995. Also sensing a connection between their beloved blues and rock and African music, singer **Robert Plant** and guitarist **Jimmy Page** of Led Zepplin fame recorded with an array of North African musicians in 1994. They dubbed the project Unledded.

JAZZ COLLABORATIONS

Jazz musicians, long aware of African elements in their music, have naturally ventured onto today's African music-scape. On the commercial side, French jazz violinist **Jean Luc Ponty** assembled a killer lineup of Paris-based African studio players for his 1991 outing, *Tchokolo*. Jean Luc himself can't plumb the depths of his players' musical backgrounds, but this record and tour served notice to his fusion following that Africa hosts some knock-out instrumentalists. More a labor of love than a commercial project, ex-Charles Mingus pianist **Don Pullen** headed the African-Brazilian Connection, featuring Senegalese percussionist **Mor Thiam**. Mor also worked with the **World Saxophone Quartet and African Drums** on the album *Metamorphosis*.

The spiritual Gnawa musicians of Morocco have also attracted jazz collaborators, including tenor sax giant **Pharoah Sanders**, who released an album with **Maleem Mahmoud Ghania** in 1994, and also pianist, composer and arranger **Randy Weston**, who has lived in Morocco and has recorded and toured with Gnawa musicians, including acclaimed European performances in 1994. Another legendary jazz pianist **Herbie Hancock** has made two intriguing records with *kora* player and singer **Foday Musa Suso**, *Village Life* and *Jazz Africa*. Bassist and producer **Bill Laswell** has collaborated with a range of North and West African artists from Moroccan rockers **Aisha Kandisha's Jarring Effects** to Foday Musa Suso. The album he made for Jajouka master **Bachir Attar**, *The Next Dream*, features tracks with **Maceo Parker**, legendary sax player of James Brown's band.

While jazz- and rock-oriented collaborations have a natural logic, few artists from the ranks of classical ensembles have approached African material. In one noteworthy exception, the adventurous **Kronos Quartet** of San Francisco produced an entire release of recordings made with African artists, *Pieces of Africa*, in 1992.

THE INTRA-AFRICAN DIALOGUE

Some of the most interesting cross-cultural projects unite musicians around the African Diaspora. **Stevie Wonder** sat in on harmonica on **King Sunny Adé's** 1984 release *Aura*. Pop reggae star **Jimmy Cliff** recorded a lyrical track with **Franco's TPOK Jazz** in Zaire in 1988, released on Cliff's 1992 album *Breakout*. One of the top-selling stars in Latin music, Dominican singer **Juan Luis Guerra**, invited Zairean *soukous* guitar star **Diblo Dibala** and vocalist **Papa Wemba** to join him on his acclaimed 1994 release *Fogaraté*. The two volumes of **Africando** brought together two generations of Senegalese singers with top Latin session players in New York for an inspired exploration of Afro-Latin traditions. **Manu Dibango** has twice assembled the top African stars of the moment for ambitious group efforts—the famine-relief appeal "Tam Tam Pour L'Ethiopie" in 1985, and his 1994 album *Wakafrika*.

Tunisia's top singer **Amina Anaabi**, now lives in Paris where she heads an adventurous band made up of French, Ethiopian, Senegalese and Tunisian musicians. The female a capella group **Zap Mama** includes five women from Africa and the Caribbean under the direction of half-Zairean, half-Belgian singer **Marie Daulne**. Their arrangements touch on everything from Marie's spiritual base—hypnotic Pygmy singing—to all-vocal renderings of reggae, zouk and medieval European polyphony. Equally unexpected, Mali's young lion of the 21-string kora **Toumani Diabate** has twice matched his musical wits with Spain's burning "new flamenco" group, **Ketama**. Collectively called **Songhai**, the group's 1988 and '94 releases freely explore the resonances between Manding griot traditions and Iberian gypsy flamenco.

Ghanaian bandleader **Nana Ampadu** once said, "Every musician is a thief in his own field." If so, much cultural loot changes hands in these musical conversations. As the '90s move on, the field gets bigger, and each encounter offers possibilities—a glorious dud, a flash in the pan, or a sound that engages its audience deeply and spins a new thread in the expanding Afropop web.

Opposite, above: Peter Gabriel with Angelique Kidjo and Branford Marsalis Opposite, below: Paul Simon Left: Zap Mama Above: Kronos Quartet with Foday Musa Suso

ACOUSTIC AND TRADITIONAL RECORDINGS DISCOGRAPHY

We have selected some recordings especially for people who appreciate acoustic music. Some are field recordings of traditional music while others are contemporary studio recodings of traditional music.

In the US., the following labels specialize in traditional/acoustic music: Smithsonian Folkways, Lyrichord, Music of the World, the Explorer Nonesuch series and Japan's JVC series distributed by Caprice in the U.S. For French labels, look for Ocora, Playasound, Unesco, and the Musique du Monde/Music from the World series on Buda. The British independent labels GlobeStyle and World Circuit have many acoustic recordings in their catalogues.

WEST AFRICA

KORA MUSIC:

(Gambia, Mali, Guinea, Senegal)

⊙ Toumani Diabate, **Kaira** (Hannibal/Rykodisc, US)

⊙ Alhaji Bai Konte, **Alhaji Bai Kante** (Rounder, US)

⊙ Dembo Konte, Kausu Kouyate & Mawdo Suso, **Ni Kanu** (Xenophile, US) • **Jaliology** (Xenophile, US)

⊙ Dembo Konte & Kausa Kouyate, **Simbomba** (Rogue, UK) • **Jali Roll** (Rogue, UK) •

⊙ Dembo Konte & Malamini Jobarteh, **Jaliya** (Stern's)

⊙ Amadu Bansang Jobarteh, **Tabara** (Music of the World, US)

⊙ Jali Musa Jawara, **Jali Musa Jawara** (Oval, UK) • Sou-

bindoor (Mango, US) • **Yasimika** (Hannibal/Rykodisc, UK)

⊙ Jali Nyama Suso, **Kora Manding** (Ocora, France)

⊙ Salieu Suso, **Griot** (Lyrichord, US)

⊙ Various, **Ancient Heart: Mandinka and Fulani Music of Gambia** (Axiom/Island, US) • **African Rhythms and Instruments, Vol. 1** (Lyrichord, US) • **Sounds of West Africa: The Kora & the Xylophone** (Lyrichord, US)

SENEGAL:

⊙ Pascal Diatta & Sona Mané, **Simnadé + 4** (Rogue, UK)

⊙ Dudu Ndiaye Rose, **Djaboté** (RealWorld, UK)

⊙ Various, **Tabala Wolof: Sufi Drumming of Senegal** (Village Pulse/Stern's) • **Tom-Tom Arabesques: The Drums of Shell Island** (JVC) • **Musique des Peul et des Tenda** (Ocora, France)

GUINEA:

⊙ Sory Kandia Kouyate, **L'Epopée du Mandingue, V.** 1-2 (Bolibana, France) • **An Anthology of the Manding Balafon, v. 1-2** (Doundoumba)

⊙ Fatala, **Timini** (RealWorld, UK)

⊙ Various, **Les Peuls du Wassolou—La Danse des Chasseurs** (Ocora, France)

⊙ Les Ballets Africains, **Les Ballets Africains** (Buda/France)

⊙ Les Ballets Africains de Papa Ladji Camara, self-titled (Lyrichord, US)

⊙ Various, **Guinée: Songs and Rhythms from the Coastal Region of Guinea** (Buda, France) • **Récits et Épopées** (Ocora, France)

MALI:

⊙ Bajourou, **Big String Theory** (Xenophile, US/GlobeStyle, UK)

⊙ Kasse Mady, **Kela Tradition** (Stern's)

⊙ Boubacar Traore, **Mariama** (Stern's Africa) • **Kar Kar** (Stern's Africa)

BURKINA FASO:

⊙ Anka Dia & Les Frères Coulibaly, **Music and Songs from Burkina Faso** (Audivis, France)

⊙ Adama Drame, **Mandingo Drums, v. 1-2** (Playasound, France)

⊙ Farafina, **Bolomokote** (Vera Bra, Germany) • **Faso Denou** (RealWorld, UK)

⊙ Koko du Burkina Faso, **Balafons & Tambours D'Afrique, v. 2** (Playasound, France)

⊙ Various, **Danses du Burkina Faso** (Buda, France) •

⊙ Various (Burkina, Mali, Niger), **Africa: Drum, Chant, and Instrumental Music** (Explorer Nonesuch, US)

NIGER:

⊙ Guem, **Compilation** (Voix D'Afrique)

⊙ Various, **Anthologie de la Musique du Niger** (Ocora, France) • **Nomades du Desert** (Playasound, France)

IVORY COAST:

⊙ Various, **Tom Tom Fantasy: Live Performance from the Mask Festival** (JVC, Japan) • **Baule Vocal Music** (Unesco/Auvidis, France) • **Masques Dan** (Ocora, France)

SIERRA LEONE:

⦿ *Various*, **Musique Traditionelles** (Ocora, France)

GHANA:

⦿ *Mustapha Tetty Addy*, **Royal Drums of Ghana**
⦿ *Obo Addy*, **Okropong** (Earthbeat, US)
⦿ *Kakraba Lobi*, **The World of Kakraba Lobi** (JVC, Japan)
⦿ *Pan-African Orchestra*, **Pan-African Orchestra** (RealWorld/Caroline, US)
⦿ *Various*, **Master Musicians of Dagbon** (Rounder, US)
• **Drum Gahu: Good-time Dance Music from the Ewe Pepole of Ghana and Togo** (White Cliffs Media, US)

TOGO:

⦿ *Various*, **Togo: Music From West Africa** (Rounder, US)

BENIN:

⦿ *Various*, **Bariba and Somba Music** (Unesco/Auvidis, France)

NIGERIA:

⦿ *Various*, **Yoruba Street Percussion** (Original Music, US)

CAPE VERDE:

⦿ *Various*, **Music from Cape Verde** (Caprice, US)

CENTRAL AND EASTERN AFRICA

MUSIC OF THE PYGMY PEOPLE (CAMEROON, ZAIRE, GABON):

⦿ *Various*, **Heart of the Forest** (Hannibal/Rykodisc, US)
• **Mbuti Pygmies of the Ituri Rainforest** (Smithsonian Folkways/Rounder, US) • **Music of the Rain Forest Pygmies** (Lyrichord, US) • **Musiques des Pygmées Bibayak** (Ocora, France)

ZAIRE:

⦿ *Various*, **Music of the Shi People, Songs Accompanied**

by **Likembe** (JVC/Caprice, Japan) • **Petites Musiques du Zaire** (Buda, France) • **Tambours Kongo** (Buda, France) ⦿ *Various*, **Zaire: Polyphonies Mongo** (Ocora, France) • **Zaire: Tombe Ditumba** (Fonti Musicali, Belgium)

BURUNDI:

⦿ *The Burundi Drummers*, **The Burundi Drummers** (RealWorld, UK)
⦿ *Various*, **Musiques Traditionelles** (Ocora, France)

TANZANIA:

⦿ *Master Musicians of Tanzania*, **Mateso (Suffering)** (Triple Earth, UK)
⦿ *Various*, **The Art of Hukwe Zawose** (JVC, Japan)

KENYA:

⦿ *Muungano National Choir*, **Missa Luba** (Philips, Netherlands)
⦿ *Ayub Ogada*, **En Mana Kuoyo** (RealWorld/Caroline, UK)
⦿ *Various*, **Songs the Swahili Sing** (Original Music, US)

SOUTHERN AFRICA

ZIMBABWE MBIRA RECORDINGS:

⦿ *Ephat Mujuru*, **Rhythms of Life** (Lyrichord, US)
⦿ *Various*, **The Soul of Mbira** (Nonesuch/Elektra, US)

MADAGASCAR:

⦿ *Bemiray*, **Polyphones des Hauts-Plateaux** (Ocora, France)
⦿ *Various*, **Possession et Poésie** (Ocora, France) • **Madagaskari 1, 2, 3** (Feuer und Eis, Germany) • **Madagascar—Musique Traditionelle du Sud-Ouest** (Pithys, France) • **Madagasikara One: Current Traditional Music of Madagascar** (GlobeStyle, UK) • **Madagasccar— Le Valiha** (Playasound, France) • **The Music of Madagascar: Classic Traditional Recordings from the 1930s** (Shanachie, US)

MOZAMBIQUE:

⦿ *Various*, **Mozambique One**, **Mozambique Two** (GlobeStyle/Rounder, US) • **Music from Mozambique, v. 1-2** (GlobeStyle, UK)

NORTH AFRICA

EGYPT:

⦿ *Various*, **Musicians of the Nile** (RealWorld/Caroline, US)

MOROCCO:

[See Gnawa section on page 62]
⦿ *Ustad Massano Tazi*, **Classique Andalouse de Fes** (Ocora, France)
⦿ *Various*, **Moyen Atlas—Musique Sacred et Profane** (Ocora, France)

ALGERIA:

⦿ *Various*, **Moyen Atlas, Musique Sacred et Profane** (Ocora, France)

ETHIOPIA:

⦿ *Seleshe Damessae*, **Tesfaye** (Music of the World, US) • **Songs from Ethiopia Today** (Welt Musik, Germany)
⦿ *Various*, **Kirar, Appolo's Harp** (JVC, Japan)

Opposite, bottom: Ghanian drums   Opposite, top: Les Ballets Africains of Guinea   Above: Toumani Diabate of Mali, playing kora   Left: Ngororombe panpipe players in Zimbabwe

SUPPLEMENTARY DISCOGRAPHY

AFRICAN COMPILATIONS

Various artists: • **African Moves, V.** 1-3 (Stern's Africa) • **Africa Never Stand Still** (3 discs & booklet) (Ellipsis Arts, US) • **30 Ans de Musique Africaine** (Sonodisc, France) • **Planet Africa: The World of African Music** (Rhythm Safari, US) • **Out of Africa** (Rykodisc, US) • **African Connection, v. 2—West Africa** (Celluloid, France) • **Mbuki Mvuki** (Original Music, US) • **Africa Dances** (Original Music, US) • **African Acoustic** Original Music, US) • **Compact D'Afrique** (GlobeStyle, UK) • **Sound D'Afrique, v.** 1-2 (Mango, US) • **Africa Fête, #**1-3 (Mango, US) • **Roots Piranha: Sound Tracks Into World Music** (Piranha, Germany) • **No Make Palaver: Very Very Music of West Africa** (Piranha, Germany) • **There's A Griot Going on...** (Rogue, UK) • **Afrique en Or** (Lusafrica, France) • **The Most Beautiful Songs of Africa** (Arc) • **Putumayo Presents the Best of World Music, v. 3: Africa** (Putumayo, US) • **Oriental Feeling** (North African focus) (RCA, France) • **Reggae Africa** (EMI Hemispere, US) • **Black Star Liner: Reggae From Africa** (Rounder, US)

SOUTHERN AFRICA

SOUTH AFRICA:

- Amaqabane, **Ntate Modise** (Sounds of Soweto, SA)
- Amaswazi Emvelo, **Thul'ulalele** (Gallo, SA)
- Freddy Gwala, **Amadamara** (KGM, SA)
- Busi Mhlongo, **Babhemu** (Stern's Africa)
- Mbogeni Ngema, **Stimela Sasezola** (Tusk, SA) • **Time to Unite** (Mango, US)
- Mthembu Queens, **Emjindini** (Rounder, US)
- O'Yaba, **One Foundation** (Shanachie, US)
- Pure Gold, **By the Rivers of Babylon** (Shanachie, US)
- Sankomota, **The Writing Is On the Wall** (CCP/EMI)
- Various, **Only the Poor Man Feel It** (EMI Hemisphere, US) • **Siya Hamba! 1950s South African Country and Small Town Sounds** (Original Music, US)

ZIMBABWE:

- Real Sounds, **Wende Zako** (Rounder, US)
- Jonah Sithole, **Chenjerera Upenyu**
- look for records/tapes by Leonard Zhakata and Ngwenya Brothers

BOTSWANA:

- Duncan Senyatso & the Kgwanyape Band (Indigo, France)

MADAGASCAR:

- Jean Emilien, **Hey Madagascar** (Mélodie, France)

MAURITIUS:

- Les Windblows, **Ça Nou Sega** (Tambour, England)
- Various, **Sega Non Stop** (Playasound, France)

ANGOLA:

- Carlos Burity, **Carolina** (Mélodie, France)
- Paulo Flores, **Coraçao Farrapo e Charry** (Discosette) • **Sassasa** (Discosette)
- Teta Lando, **Esperanças Idosas** (Sonodisc, France)

- Andre Mingas, **Andre Mingas** (Valentin de Carvalho/EMI)
- Filipe Mukenga, **Kianda Kianda** (Lusafrica, France)

CENTRAL AND EAST AFRICA

ZAIRE/CONGO:

- Mbilia Bel, **Boya Ye** (Genidia/Stern's)
- Mbilia Bel/Rigo Star, **8/10 Bénedicta**
- Bella-Bella, **Bella-Bella Des Freres Soki 1970-73** (Sonodisc, France)
- Ya Ntesa Dalienst & Le Maquisard, **Belalo** (Sango/Sonodisc, France)
- Franco, Sam Mangwana et le T.P.O.K. Jazz, self-titled, (Sonodisc, France)
- Franco & Rochereau, **Omona Wapi** (Shanachie, US)
- Shaba Kahamba, **Bitumba** (Karac/Sonodisc, US)
- Lokua Kanza, **Lokua Kanza** (Night & Day, France)
- Pablo Lubadika, **Okominiokolo** (Stern's Africa)
- Lubumbashi Stars du Zaire, **S.O.S. Passe Partout** (Sonodisc, France)
- Jean-Bosco Mwenda (Mwenda wa Bayeke), **African Guitar Legend** (Rounder, US)
- Theo Blaise Nkounkou, **Les Plus Grands Succes, v.** 1-3
- Papa Noel, **No No** (Gefraco, France)
- Nouvelle Génération de la République Démocratique, **Sasa La Graisse!** (Sonodisc, France)
- Nyboma, **Anicet** (Stern's Africa, US)
- Koffi Olomide, **Tcha Tcho** (Stern's Africa) * **Haut de Gamme** (Sonodisc, France) * **Magie**
- Rochereau & l'Afrisa International, **1973-1976** (Sonodisc, France)
- Tabu Ley Rochereau, **Baby Pancake** (African Music Gallery, US)
- Soukous Stars, **Gozando** (Mélodie, France/Stern's Africa, US-UK) • **Soukous Attack** (African Music Gallery, US)
- Soukous Vibration, **Vol. 2, Souvenirs des Anées '59 à '67** (Sonodisc, France)
- Super Stars, **Marie Mozege** (Stern's Africa)
- Madilu System, **Sans Commentaire** (Stern's)
- T.P.O.K. Jazz w/Dalienst, **Belalo** (Sonodisc, France)
- Bibi Dens Tshibayi, **The Best Ambience** (Rounder, US)
- Antoine Wendo, **Nani Akolela Wendo?** (Sowarex, Belgium)
- Wenge Musica BCBG, **Les Anges Adorable, v. 2** (Sonodisc, France)
- Various, **Super Guitar Soukous** (EMI Hemisphere, US)

CENTRAL AFRICAN REPUBLIC:

- Patience Dabany, **Levekisha** (Hemisphere, US)

GABON:

- Pierre Akendengue, **Piroguier** (Mélodie, France) • **Passé Composé** (Mélodie, France) • **Silence** (Mélodie, France)
- Oliver N'Goma, **Bane** (Noli Productions, France)

UGANDA:

- Geoffrey Oryema, **Exile** (RealWorld/Caroline, UK)

- Samite, **Pearl of Uganda** (Shanachie, US) • **Abaana Bakesa: Dance My Children Dance** (Shanachie)
- Various, **The Kampala Sound** (Original Music, US)

RWANDA:

- Cécile Kayirebwa, **Rwanda** (GlobeStyle, UK)

MALAWI:

- Alan Namoko & Chimru Jazz (Pamtondo, UK)

RÉUNION:

- Granmoun Lele, **Namouniman** (Indigo, France)
- Ziskakan, **Ziskakan** (Mango, US)

MAURITIUS:

- Jean-Claude, **Les Meilleurs Segas de Jean-Claude** (Sonodisc, France)

WEST AFRICA

SENEGAL:

- Bu-Baca Diop, **Stand** (Stern's Africa)
- Vieux Diop (Via Jo), **Vieux Diop** (Triloka Records, US)
- Orchestre Baobab, **Pirate's Choice** (World Circuit, UK) • **On Verra Ça** (World Circuit, UK) • **Bamba** (Stern's Africa)
- Étoile de Dakar, **Xalis** (Popular African Music, Germany)
- Étoile 2000, **Dakar Sound Vol. 1** (Semaphore, Netherlands)
- Touré Kunda, **Natalia** (Celluloid, France) • **Gorée** (Celluloid, France)

GAMBIA:

- Ifang Bondi, **Daraja** (MW Records, Holland)

GUINEA BISSAU:

- Kaba Mane, **Best of...** (Mélodie, France)
- N'Kassa Cobra, **Lundju** (Lusafrica/Mélodie, France)
- Ramiro Naka, **Salvador** (Mango, US)
- Tino Trimó, **Kambalacho** (MB Records, US)

MALI:

- Super Biton du Mali, **Afro Jazz du Mali** (Shanachie, US)
- Zani Diabate, **Zani Diabate** (Mango, US)
- Kasse Mady, **Fode** (Stern's)
- Mangala, **Complainte Mandingue Blues** (Babadan/Night & Day, France)
- Various, **Electric & Acoustic Mali** (EMI Hemisphere, US)

NIGER:

- Saadou Bori & Moussa Poussy, **Niamey Twice** (Stern's Africa)

GUINEA:

- Les Amazones de Guinée, **Au Coeur de Paris** (Bolibana/Mélodie, France)
- Sona Diabate, **Kankele Ti**
- Djeli Moussa Diawara (also spelled Jali Musa Jawara), **Cimadon** (Celluloid/Mélodie, France)
- Baba Djan, **Kan Kan** (Sonodisc, France)
- Go & Koteba, **Les Go de Koteba** (Mélodie, France)

● Sekouba Kandia Kouyate, self-titled, (Sonodisc, France)
● Ousmane Kouyate Band, **Domba** (Stern's)
● Kanté Manfila, **Tradition** (Mélodie, France) • **N'na Niwalé** (Popular African Music, Germany)
● Momo "Wandel" Soumah, **Matchowe** (Doundoumba, France)
● S.N.Thiam & Sékou Condé, **Guinée Dimension 93/94** (Ledoux Records/Mélodie, France)

SIERRA LEONE:
● King Masco, **From Africa With Love** (Vetma)
● Abdul T.J.'s Rokoto, **Rokoto** (Rogue, UK) • **Fire Dembolo** (Rogue, UK)
● Various, **African Elegant: Sierra Leone's Kru/Krio Connection** (Original Music, US)

IVORY COAST:
● Nyanka Bell, **Visa** (RFO/Sonodisc, France)
● Ismael Isaac, **Rahman** (Buda, France)

GHANA:
● Jewel Ackah, **Onipa Dasani** (Arsona, UK)
● Eric Agyeman, **Highlife Safari** (Stern's Africa)
● Super Sweet Talks, **The Lord's Prayer** (Stern's Africa)
● Dr. K. Gyasi & His Noble Kings, **Sikyi Highlife '92** (Noble King, Ghana)

BENIN:
● Gnonnas Pedro, **La Compilation, V. 1-2** (Ledoux Records/Mélodie, France)
● Ignace de Souza, **The Great Unknowns** (Original Music, US)

NIGERIA:
● King Sunny Adé, **The Return of the Juju Master** (Mercury, US)
● Admiral Dele Abiodun, **Adawa Super Sound** (Shanachie, US) • **Confrontation** (Earthworks/Stern's, US)
● Gaspar Lawal, **Kadara** (GlobeStyle, UK)
● Babatunde Olatunji, **Drums of Passion** (Columbia, US) [Also look for cassettes by Haruna Ishola, Fabulous Olu Fajemirokun, Orlando Owoh, Wasiu Ayinde Marshal, Queen Salawa Abeni, Abass Akande Obesere, Chief Wasiu Alabi, Dayo Kujore, Timi Osukoya, and Dele Taiwo.]

CAPE VERDE:
● Bau, **Jaílza** (Lusafrica/Mélodie, France)
● Os Conquistadores, **Traidora** (Lusafrica, France)
● Homero Andrade Os Conquistadores, **Chica** (Lusafrica, France)
● Gardenia, **Mix II** (MB Records, US)
● Mendes Brothers, **Palonkon** (MB Records, US)
● Mindel Band, **Mindelo** (Lusafrica, France)
● Mirri Lobo, **Paranoia** (MB Records, US)
● Nova Estrella, **Amigo Bedjo** (Sonodics, France)
● Tam Tam 2000, **Sabe Cabo Verde** (Lusafrica, France)
● Titina, **Titina Sings B. Leza—Music of Cape Verde** (Mélodie, France)
● Tito Pares, **Dança Ma Mi Criola** (MB Records, US)
● Os Tubarões, **Portons D'Nós Ilha** (Lusafrica, France)
● Various, **Cape Verde: Anthology 1959-1992** (Buda, France) • **Cape Verde Islands—The Roots** (Playasound, France) • **World Beat—Vol. 6, Cabo Verde** (Celluloid, France)

CAMEROON:
● Moni Bile, **Chagrin D'Amour** (Touré Jim's Records/Sonodisc, France)

● Ben Decca & Puissance 7, **Ben Decca & Puissance 7** (TJR Music/Sonodisc, France)
● Sissy Dipoko, **Munan** (JBC, France)
● Penda Dalle, **Alea Mba** (Sonodisc, France)
● Henri Dikongué, **Wa** (Buda/Mélodie, France)
● Douleur, **Beneground** (Kanibal, France)
● Emile Kangue, **Jombe Di Telame** (TJR Music/Sonodisc, France)
● Alex Mouna, **Time Ni Time** (Sonodisc, France)
● Petit Pays, **Best of...** (Mélodie, France)
● Georges Seba, **Lions Indomptables** (Sonodisc, France)
● Various, **Fleurs Musicales du Cameroun** (FMC, Cameroon)

NORTHERN AFRICA

EGYPT:
● Farid el Atrache, **The Best of...** (Voice of Lebanon, Lebanon) • **King of the Oud** (Voice of Lebanon, Lebanon) • **For Ever, V. 1-2** (EMI Greece)
● Abdu Dagir, **Malik At-Taqasim** (Enja, Germany)
● Hossam Ramzy and his Egyptian Ensemble, **Egyptian Rai** (ARC Music, US/UK/Germany) • **Source of Fire** (ARC Music, US/UK/Germany)
● Mokhtar al Said, **Raks Sharki: Classic Egyptian Dance Music** (Piranha, Germany)
● Salamat, **Salam Delta** (Piranha, Germany)
● Hassan abu Seoud & Orchestra, **Belly Dances from the Middle-East** (Sonodisc, France)
● Warda, **Madritouche** (Blue Silver/Mélodie, France) • **Batwans Beek** (Aalem al Fin, Egypt) • **Ismaauni** (Fassiphone, Morocco) [Warda is originally from Morocco]

TUNISIA:
● Amarna, **Maaquila** (Aladin, France)
● Amina Annabi, **Wa Di Yé** (Philips, France)
● Fawzi Ben Gamra, **Bint Al Hellel** (Phonie, Tunisia) • **Najibik Najibik** (Phonie, Tunisia)
● Elhadi Habuba, **Rim Zamini** (Audiophone, Tunisia)
● Latifa, **Hubik Hedi** (Larein, Tunisia)
● Amina Nakht, **Mahasaltish** (Soca, Tunisia)
● Various, **Tunis Chante et Danse (1900-1950)** (Alif, France)

ALGERIA:
● Alla, **Foundou from Bechar** (Al Sur, France)
● Mohand Azar, **Rock Habile** (Aladin Le Musicien, France)
● Djurdura, **Le Defi** (France)
● Ait Menguellet, **Awkni Xdarabbi** (France) • **Tselimer Fellawen** (France)
● Rachid Taha, **Rachid Taha** (Barclay, France)

MOROCCO:
● Ahlam, **Revolt Against Reason** (Barbarity, Switzerland) • **Acting Salam** (Barbarity, Switzerland)
● Hamid Baroudi, **City No Mad** (Barbarity, Switzerland)
● Samira Said, **Samira** (Adouaa Almadina, France) • **El Jani Bad Liumin** (Muriphon, Egypt)
● Latifa Arfat, **Jebel Atlas** (Adouaa A1 Madina, Morocco)
● Various, **Moroccan Street Music** (Lyrichord, US) [Also look for releases by Abdelwahab Doukali]
● Randy Weston, **Gnawa Musicians of Morocco featuring Randy Weston** (Verve, Polygram)

CROSS-CULTURAL RECORDINGS

● Youssou N'Dour & Neneh Cherry, **7 Seconds** on **The Guide** (Colombia/USA)
● Deep Forest, **Deep Forest** (Sony, Japan)
● Paul Simon, **Graceland** (Warner, US) • **The Rhythm of the Saints** (Warner, US)
● Peter Gabriel, **Passion** (RealWorld, UK)
● Henry Kaiser, David Lindley et al, **A World Out of Time, v. 1-2** (Shanachie, US)
● Robert Plant and Jimmy Page, **No Quarter** (Atlantic)
● Ali Farka Toure with Ry Cooder, **Talking Timbuktu** (World Circuit, UK/Hannibal/Rykodisc, US)
● Jean Luc Ponty, **Tchokolo** (Epic, US)
● Don Pullen and the Afro-Brazilian Connection, **Kele Mou Bana** (Blue Note, US)
● Maleem Mahmoud Ghania w/Pharoah Sanders, **The Trance of Seven Colors** (Axiom/Island, US)
● Randy Weston, **Gnawa Musicians of Morocco featuring Randy Weston** (Verve, Polygram)
● Herbie Hancock & Foday Musa Suso, **Jazz Africa** (Verve/Polygram, US) • **Village Life** (Sony, Japan)
● Foday Musa Suso, **The Dreamtime** (CMP, US)
● World Saxophone Quartet w/African Drums, **Metamorphosis** (Nonesuch/Elektra, US)
● Art Ensemble of Chicago w/Amabutho, **Art Ensemble of Soweto** (DIW, US)
● King Sunny Ade, **Aura** (Island, US)
● Jimmy Cliff, **Breakout** (JRS, US)
● Juan Luis Guerra, **Fogaraté** (Karen, US)
● Africando, **Trovador** (Stern's Africa) • **Tierra Tradicional** (Stern's Africa)
● Kronos Quartet, **Pieces of Africa** (Nonesuch/Elektra, US)
● Amina Annabi, **Yalil** (Mango, US) • **Wa Di Yé** (Philips)
● Zap Mama, **Adventures in Afropea** (Luaka Bop/Warner, US) • **Sabsylma** (Luaka Bop/Warner, US)
● Songhai (Toumani Diabate, Ketama, Danny Thompson) (Hannibal/Rykodisc, US) • **Songhai 2** (Hannibal/Rykodisc, US)

GLOSSARY OF MUSICAL TERMS

African Jazz: South Africa's unique blend of American jazz instrumentation and arrangement concepts with indigenous sources such as marabi. Many African groups such as Guinea's Bembeya Jazz and Zaire's T.P.O.K. Jazz incorporated "jazz" in band names but did not have the same direct connection to American jazz as did the groups in South Africa.

afrobeat: Term coined by Nigerian iconoclast Fela Anikulapo-Kuti for his fusion of West African and black American music.

Afropop: Contemporary African music in its wide variety. Usually refers to urban, electric dance music. Sometimes mistakenly used to signify one style or sound. Also refers to AFROPOP series launched in 1988 on National Public Radio in the US.

agooda: Sierra Leone street music popularized by Abdul T-Jay.

al-jeel: Literally "the new wave," this modern Egyptian dance music originally created by Egyptians and Libyan expatriates in Cairo, is a favorite among middle class youth. Fusion of Nubian, Bedouin and Egyptian rhythms.

Andalous: From Andalusia, the region of southern Spain ruled by the Moors until late in the 15th century, and renowned for its highly developed classical music tradition. Today, Andalous music survives mostly in Morocco.

ambass-bey: Cameroonian street music popularized by Salle John and others.

apala: Yoruba vocal and percussion music from Nigeria popularized by the late Haruna Ishola.

asiko: Popular music sung in the Yoruba language in Nigeria during the 1920s and 1930s. Important influence on development of juju.

authenticité: French for "authenticity." Era-shaping policy decreed by Mobutu in early '70s Zaire to discourage European and colonial-era identity and to encourage indigenous sources in names, dress and culture. Franco played a key role in spreading the word about authenticité to the masses.

Axé: Yoruba word roughly translatable as "life force," now applied as a label for the Afro-Bahian pop style of Brazil becoming increasingly popular in that country.

balafon: West African xylophone made of wood.

batá: Family of three double-headed Nigerian drums played across the lap. Used in the Yoruba religious music of Cuba.

bendir: Northern African hand drum constructed from a circular wooden frame, 40-50 cm. across, with a taut skin stretched over it. Used in many forms of traditional and modern music from this region.

benga: Musical style from western Kenya originally from the Luo people but now more widely used throughout the country.

biguine: Dance rhythm from Martinique.

bikutsi: Popular Cameroonian folk-based rhythm and pop style with a triplet feel from the Yaoundé area.

bolero: Slow ballad, popular in Cuba, Puerto Rico and Mexico.

boucher: Popular Congolese dance, first introduced by Les Bantous de la Capitale of Brazzaville in 1965.

box guitar: Common African term for an acoustic guitar.

cavacha: Zairian dance rhythm popular in the '70s.

chachachá: Cuban style, very popular internationally in '50s and still popular in Cuba today. The first chachachá was by Enrique Jorrín called "La Engañadora."

charanga: Cuban orchestra with violins, flutes, timbales, piano, and unison singing. Charangas led by Johnny Pacheco and others were very popular in Africa in the '60s.

cheb/chebba: Young man/young woman. Algerian and Moroccan rai singers began using these titles in the '70s as a proud assertion of their youth, and of their music's commitment to the concerns of youth.

cheikh/cheikha: Titles conferring honor upon male and female popular singers in pre-independence Algeria. Singing classical poetry and love songs, cheikhs and cheikhas preceded the bolder chebs and chabas of rai music.

chemko: The fast, final section of a Tanzanian dance band tune; analogous to the seben in Zairean music.

chimurenga: In Shona, means "struggle." Describes the mbira-based music of Thomas Mapfumo and others from Zimbabwe.

clave: Pair of polished hardwood sticks struck together to produce a high-pitched sound. Also refers to the two-bar rhythmic pattern underlying Afro-Cuban music, incor-

porated into early Congolese music.

condamble: Afro-Brazilian syncretic religion. Venerates the Yoruba pantheon and incorporates Bantu elements.

conga: Single-headed barrel-shaped drum of West African descent. Played in virtually all Latin bands.

Congo music: Widely used term in Africa for dance music from Zaire and the Congo.

didadi: Athletic dance rhythm from Wassoulou region of Mali.

disco: Generic term used for a music style popular in South African townships from the early '80s to the present, characterized by keyboards and heavy dance beat. Sometimes called "bubblegum."

djembe: West African hand drum often with metal sheets attached to add buzz and project its sharp sound.

dry guitar: Common African term for acoustic guitar.

firquah: Egyptian film orchestra consisting of traditional North African instruments and, from the '20s on, violins and other western instruments.

fuji: Yoruba voice and percussion style popularized by Sikiru Ayinde Barrister and Alhaji Ayinla Kollington. Currently very popular in Nigeria.

funana: Cape Verdean dance, typically with accordion and metal scraper.

gimbri: Common North African lute of sub-Saharan origin. Characteristics include a round, fretless neck, two or three strings, and a sound box with a drum-like hide face. Also called sintir.

Gnawa: Spiritual brotherhood in Morocco of people descended from slaves brought from Mali in the 16th century. Gnawa music—featuring two- or three-string sintir or gimbri, unison singing and hand clapping—is played at healing ceremonies.

goje or goge: West African single stringed instrument, making a sound like the violin.

griot/griotte: French words for male "jali" and female "jalimusolu," the traditional bards of the Manding diaspora responsible for keeping oral histories and family lineages. Plays instruments such as kora and balafon.

gospel highlife: Highlife music with Christian themes played in the churches of Ghana.

Now one of the biggest selling styles of music in the country.

groaner: South African male singer who takes deep bass part in mbaqanga songs. The most famous groaner is Mahlathini.

highlife: Dance music from Ghana and eastern Nigeria. Very popular in West Africa in the '40s, '50s and '60s.

indlamu: Traditional zulu dance where the dancer lifts one foot over his head and brings it down hard, landing squarely on the downbeat. Typically, two dancers in warrior's pelts perform indlamu routines together, shadowing each other's moves perfectly.

iscathamiya: South African acapella singing style popularized internationally by Ladysmith Black Mambazo.

iskista: Ethiopian dance involving shaking shoulders and heaving chests. Very popular in Addis Ababa beerhalls.

jali: Court or wandering bard in Manding society responsible for keeping oral histories and family lineages. Plays instruments such as kora and balafon.

jalimusolu: Female griot singer in West Africa

jit: Vocal and percussion music from Zimbabwe, modernized by Bhundu Boys, James Chimombe and others.

jive: South African urban electric pop music.

juju: Popular Yoruba style from Nigeria, featuring talking drums, guitars, keyboards, and sometimes pedal steel. The first modern juju star was I.K. Dairo. Top-selling juju star and international popularizer is King Sunny Adé.

kabosy: Traditional four-stringed guitar-like instrument from Madagascar, played by Dama, Rossy and others. Plays lively, strummed rhythms.

kalindula: Zambian pop music style. Originally named after a traditional one-string bass, kalindula has become a general term for much of this southern African country's homegrown pop.

kamele ngoni: Literally "young person's harp." A smaller version of the doso ngoni, or "hunter's harp," this six-string harplute gives the Wassoulou music of southern Mali distinctive, funky, low lines that define its rhythm and harmony.

kiri kiri: Dance rhythm popularized by the late Doctor Nico in Zaire in mid-'60s.

kora: 21-string harp-lute played in Mali, the Gambia, Guinea, and Senegal. Central to Manding culture.

kpanlogo: Popular percussion rhythm developed in Ghana in the '60s.

krar: Ancient Ethiopian lyre with five or six gut or nylon strings. A krar has a bowl-shaped, goatskin-covered resonator as well as a large wooden yoke held in place by two wooden arms. Sometimes called Harp of Apollo.

kwassa kwassa: Dance popular in Zaire in the late '80s. Used by Kanda Bongo Man to describe his music.

kwela: Pennywhistle street music from South Africa, starting in the '50s.

likembe: Thumb piano from Zaire.

Lingala: Trade language along Zaire River between present-day Congo and Zaire. The language used in modern soukous music.

maalimi: Master of a brotherhood of musicians, specifically the famed Jajouka group from the Moroccan village of Jajouka in the foothills of the Atlas Mountains.

madiaba: Zairian dance craze in the late '80s that succeeded kwassa kwassa.

Maghreb: The westernmost part of the Arabic-speaking world, the Maghreb stretches from Egypt west across northern Africa to the Atlantic Ocean, Morocco being its furthest extremity.

makassi: Rhythm popularized by Cameroonian star Sam Fan Thomas whose hits were key to launching the international makossa boom in the mid-'80s.

makossa: Cameroonian dance rhythm from Douala area. Also the name of the country's most successful pop style.

makozouk: Fusion of makossa and zouk made primarily by Cameroonian composers and producers in Paris.

malhoun: Semi-classical poetry and music tradition dating back to the Moorish settlement of Andalusia in southern Spain.

mambo: Afro-Cuban musical form that became popular in the US during the '50s. Mambo also refers to an instrumental section of a salsa or merengue tune.

Manding: Term used to describe a widespread West African language group and the associated music culture.

maqam: One of approximately 120 scales used in Arab classical music and its popular descendants. Modern Arab music mostly uses about 20 maqams, sometimes moving through several in a single piece.

marabenta: Urban party in Mozambique featuring live music. Also a pepped up version of local majika rhythm.

marabi: South African style of piano based music played in World War I era slums. Later incorporated by emerging South African jazz bands from the '30s on. Term used loosely in South Africa to refer to various pre-electric music styles.

marovany: Deep-toned box zither from the southern part of Madagascar.

masenqo: Ethiopian one-string fiddle with a diamond-shaped sound box covered with goatskin.

mawal: Improvised vocals used in Egyptian shaabi music, the toast of Cairo's working class neighborhoods. Mawal lets the singer show off storytelling abilities and street smarts.

mbalax: Percussion music from Senegal, modernized by Youssou N'Dour and others.

mbaqanga: South African township music popular from the mid-'60s to mid-'70s.

mbira: Thumb piano of the Shona people in Zimbabwe. Played by plucking metal strips fixed to a wooden slab, often clamped inside a gourd resonator. Used recreationally and to communicate with ancestors.

mbube: Term used generally to describe South African Zulu choral music. First used in the 1930s to describe the gospel-oriented sound of Solomon Linda, author of famous song "Mbube."

merdoum: Folkloric vocal and drum style made popular by Sudanese singer and bandleader Abdel Gadir Salim.

merengue: High-energy dance beat from the Dominican Republic, very popular throughout the Latin world. Essential percussion instruments are a tambora and gúira, with congas added in modern bands. Originally featuring accordion, today's bands have keyboards and brass with fast repeated saxophone patterns.

milo jazz: Sierra Leone street music named after Milo malt drink.

mi-solo: In Zairean three-part guitar arrangements, the one that plays between the lead and the rhythm guitar, sometimes adapting either of their roles.

morna: Song form from Cape Verde characterized by sad, often minor-key emotional tone.

montuno: Section of an Afro-Cuban dance tune using call-and-response between improvisations by the lead singer and repeated phrases by a vocal chorus.

mqashiyo: What Mahlathini and the Mahotella Queens in South Africa first called their style of mbaqanga.

mtindo: In Tanzania, the musical and performance style of each band and the dancing style associated with it.

mutuashi: Dance and rhythm from southern Zaire popularized by Tshala Muana.

njarka: From Mali, small bowed fiddle made from a gourd with long neck and one thin gut string.

ngoma: Refers to a combination of music/song/dance in Tanzania and Kenya. Also refers to a specific type of drum, or drums in general.

Nubia: Region of the Nile valley linking Egypt and Sudan, much of it flooded to create the Aswan Dam and Lake Nasser. As Nubians have moved into major cities, their music has developed into urban styles and has influenced Cairo's al-jeel sound.

nyatiti: Seven-stringed lyre played in western Kenya.

orutu: One-stringed fiddle played in western Kenya. Also refers to currently popular Kenyan style which includes this instrument.

oud: Arabic lute consisting of a large, wooden sound box, a small fretless neck, and usually six paired strings with a single bass string.

pachanga: Fast Afro-Cuban dance rhythm popularized in New York in the late 50s. Also popular in Africa.

palm wine: Acoustic guitar music from English-speaking West Africa, associated with palm wine drink.

pata pata: South African township dance of the '50s. Song of same name became an international hit by Miriam Makeba.

polihet: Traditional girls' dance in the Ivory Coast popularized by Gnaoré Djimi whose music has a driven triplet feel and boisterous percussion breaks.

rai: Popular youth-oriented music from Algeria. Rai's themes of love and drink have brought rai singers in direct conflict with Islamic militants in Algeria.

raks sharki: Dance and music from Egypt performed at weddings and for the public in Cairo clubs. Referred to abroad as "belly dance music."

reggae: Internationally played pop style dominated by bass, drums, and rhythm guitar chops, originally from Jamaica. Originally associated with Rastafarian religion and liberation politics.

rumba: Zairean dance music of Franco's generation, influenced by Cuban music. Precursor of soukous. Rumba also refers to Afro-Cuban street drumming and dancing form.

sabar: Senegalese drum played with stick and hand, featured in many Senegalese pop bands. Also refers to an intricate percussion style involving multiple sabar drums.

salegy: Fast dance music with a triplet feel from the coast of Madagascar.

salsa: New York Puerto Rican adaptation of Afro-Cuban music that became popular during the late '60s and continues to be played in New York, Miami and the Caribbean. It has also enjoyed something

of a comeback in West Africa.

samba: The basic rhythm which underpins Brazilian popular music in many varieties.

samba-reggae: Brazilian version of reggae, developed in Salvador by the bloco afro Olodum.

sambista: Person who plays or dances samba.

Santería: Yoruba-derived Afro-Cuban religion celebrated with music and dance. Also called lucumí.

Sapeurs: Stylishly dressed members of the Society of Ambienceurs and Persons of Elegance. Spearheaded by Papa Wemba and other Zairean celebrities but picked up by other Africans living in Paris and around the world.

sax jive: South African township dance music in '60s which developed from "penny-whistle jive." See also kwela.

seben: Fast, final section of the modern Zairian song form.

semba: Angolan dance, the antecedent of Brazilian samba.

shaabi: Working-class pop music of Cairo. Surged in popularity with the advent of the cassette revolution in the early '70s.

Shango: Trinidadian religion drawn from Yoruba tradition. Shango drumming has influenced modern soca rhythm.

shebeen: Illegal drinking establishment that sold liquor to black South Africans. Musical performances also took place in shebeens.

sintir: Large plucked-string lute played by Gnawa musicians, mostly in Morocco. The instrument has two or three strings, a drum-like sound box, and a removable resonator that adds a buzzing sound to its low, resonant notes.

spraying: Term used in west Africa for showing appreciation of a musician by placing money on them while performing. Lucrative additional source of income for musicians. Also called dashing.

soca: Modern Trinidadian pop music. Word comes from combining "soul" and "calypso."

son: An Afro-Cuban musical form that evolved in Cuba's rural Oriente province. Very popular during the '20s, it formed the basis for much of Cuba's music and had an enormous influence on Central Africa's popular music as well.

soukous: Generic term for modern Zairean dance music.

soundama: Dance craze in Zaire, based on folk music.

Swahili: Language widely spoken in East Africa. Also refers to the Islamic Swahili people who live along the Kenyan and Tanzanian coast of East Africa.

tama: Senegambian talking drum, capable of imitating the Wolof language. Featured in electric groups of Youssou N'Dour and Baaba Maal.

tassou: Currently popular Senegalese rap style.

ukabonga: Quick, staccato rap that occurs near the middle of a typical Zulu traditional pop tune. The singer may praise his clan or family or expand on the theme of the song.

valiha: Zither, national instrument of Madagascar, similar in sound to the West African kora.

Voudou: Afro-Haitian religion with influences from West Africa, the Congo River region, and from Catholicism.

Wassoulou: Region of southeastern Mali and adjacent parts of Guinea and Ivory Coast. People are originally Fulani but now speak Bambara. Also refers to contemporary acoustic music style from this region championed by women singers such as Oumou Sangare.

Yoruba: Language and people of southwestern Nigeria. Highly developed pre-colonial civilization. Yoruba Diaspora resulting from slave trade profoundly influenced cultures of Brazil, Cuba, Haiti and elsewhere.

zekete zekete: Dance popularized by Zaiko Langa Langa in the mid-'80s.

ziglibithy: Traditional Ivorian rhythm modernized by the late Ernesto Djedje.

zomgquashiyo: Mbaqanga style associated with Mahotella Queens.

zouglou: Pop music movement in Ivory Coast which gave voice to student protest in early '90s.

zouk: Creole slang word for "party." Modern hi-tech Antillean music produced mostly in Paris. Very influential in Africa in terms of sound, production and concert presentation style.

RESOURCES DIRECTORY

Listed below are sources for recordings, information and further reading. The publisher regrets that there is insufficient space to list all of the recommendations provided by the authors. For further information, contact World Music Productions at the address listed on page IX.

COMPANIES THAT DO MAIL ORDER

USA

Stern's US
598 Broadway, 7th Floor
New York, NY 10012
(T) 212.925.1648
Major importer—Mélodie, Sonodisc, Syllart, World Circuit, KAZ, Piranha, as well as Stern's, Stern's Africa, and Stern's Earthworks

Qualiton Imports
24-02 40th Ave.
Long Island City, NY 11101
(T) 718-937-8515
Send $5.00 and specify their "non-classical" catalogue-

Africassette
P.O. Box 24941
Detroit, MI 48224
(T) 313.881.4108
Imports cassettes from Africa, especially West Africa

Original Music
RD1, Box 190
Lasher Road
Tivoli NY 12583
(T) 914.756.2767
Good compilations of African oldies and eclectic mail order service

World Music Productions
328 Flatbush Avenue, Suite 288
Brooklyn, NY 11238
Write to request merchandise brochure—Afropop t-shirts, books and live concert recordings, etc.

Irresistible Rhythms, Inc.
Route 1, Box 1320
Buckingham, VA 23921
(T) 800.969.5269
(F) 804.969.1493
Specializes in African Pop, Caribbean, Cajun-Zydeco and Latin Music

Rashid Sales Company
191 Atlantic Ave.
Brooklyn NY 11201
(T) 718.852.3295
Arabic music & video; good selection of Egyptian music

Lyrichord
141 Perry St.
New York NY 10014
(T) 212.929.8234
Traditional music from around the world

Roundup Records
P.O. Box 154
N. Cambridge MA 02140
(T) 617.661.6308
Rounder Group & many imports & domestic labels

World Music Institute
49 W. 27 St.
New York NY 10001
(T) 212.545.7536
Specializes in traditional/acoustic

Arhoolie Records Inc.
10341 San Pablo Ave.
El Cerrito CA 94530
(T) 510.525.7471
Wide-ranging mail order selections

Down Home Music
6921 Stockton Ave.
El Cerrito CA 94530
(T) 510.525.2129
Retail & mail order

UK

N.A.T.A.R.I.
23 Maybridge Square
Goring By Sea
West Sussex
Great Britain BN12 6HL
Mail order only—good selection of imported African cassettes

THE NETHERLANDS

Roots Mail Music
P.O. Box 1199
4801 BD Breda
HOLLAND
(T) 011.31.76.222235
(F) 011.31.76.200201
The most reliable mail order service in Holland specializing in African and world music, but also blues, r&b, reggae, ska, soul, roots rock & pop, gospel, zydeco and cajun

RECORD COMPANIES

USA

Stern's US
598 Broadway, 7th Floor
New York, NY 10012

Mango
Worldwide Plaza
825 8th Avenue
New York, NY 10019
Excellent world music roster

Rykodisc/Hannibal
Shetland Park
27 Congress Street
Salem, MA 01970

Xenophile
43 Beaver Brook Road
Danbury, CT 06810

Shanachie Records
37 East Clinton Street
Newton NJ 07860
Good licensed imports, US-based world music, reggae

Rounder Records Group
One Camp Street
Cambridge MA 02140
Also distributes Heartbeat and Messidor

Caroline Records
114 W. 26 St.
New York NY 10001
Distributes RealWorld

Axiom Records
Worldwide Plaza
825 8th Avenue
New York, NY 10019

Luaka Bop
Box 652
Cooper Station, NY 10276

Reach Out International Records
611 Broadway
New York NY 10012
Releases available on cassette only

UK

GlobeStyle
48-50 Steele Road
London NW10 7AS

World Circuit Records
106 Cleveland Street
London W1P 5DP

Triple Earth
116 Whitfield St.
London W1P 5RW

Stern's
116 Whitfield Street
London W1P 5RW
Mail order for UK residents; US residents—see Stern's US

RealWorld
Millside, Mill Lane, Box
Wiltshire SN14 9PN

FRANCE

Cobalt
5 rue Paul Bert
93581 St. Ouen

BUDA Musique
188 Blvd Voltaire
75011 Paris

Blue Silver and Totem
45 rue de Belleville
75019 Paris
North African specialists

Celluloid/Mélodie
50 rue Stendhal
75020 Paris

Sonodisc
85 rue Fondary
75015 Paris

Gefraco
25 rue Bergere
75009 Paris

GERMANY

Piranha Records
Carmerstr. 11
D- 10623 Berlin

Popular African Music
Damaschkeanger 51
D- 60488 Frankfurt

BELGIUM

Crammed Discs
43 Rue Général Patton
1050 Brussels

SOUTH AFRICA

Gallo
P.O. Box 2445
Johannesburg 2000
South Africa

Tusk Music Co. (Pty) LTD
P.O. Box 156
Crown Mines
Johannesburg 2025

ZIMBABWE

Gramma Records
P.O. Box ST 21 Southerton
Harare Drive Ardbennie
Harare, Zimbabwe

RECORD STORES

USA

Check world music sections in **Tower** *and* **HMV** *stores around the country and international music section at Borders.*

MultiKulti
375 West Broadway
New York, NY 10012

Sarafina Records, Inc.
787 Ninth Avenue
New York, NY 10019

Record Mart
Times Square subway stop
New York, N.Y.
Underground, ask when you get there. Latin music specialists—ask for Harry

Sound Of Market
1227 Chestnut St. 2nd FL
and 15 S. 11th St. 2nd FL
Philadelphia PA
19104/19107

Paul's CD's
4526 Liberty Avenue
Bloomfield, PA 15224

Record Village
5519 Walnut Street.
Pittsburgh, PA 15232

Plan 9
1325 W. Main Street
Charlottesville, VA 22903

Town & Campus Records
20 W. Water Street
Harrisonburg, VA 22801

Horizons Records
347 S. Pleasantburg Dr.
Greenville, SC 29607

Ear-Xtacy Records
1534 Bardstown Road
Louisville, KY 40205

Erwin Music
52 1/2 Wentworth St.
Charleston, SC 29401

Blue Note Records
16401 NE 15 Avenue
North Miami Beach, FL
33162

Rankin Records
164 NE 167rd Street
North Miami Beach, FL
33162

Streetside Records
6314 Delmar Blvd.
St. Louis, MO 63130

Vintage Vinyl
6610 Delmar Blvd.
St. Louis, MO 63130

West End Wax
389 N. Euclid Ave.
St. Louis, MO 63108

Wax n'Facts
432 Morland Avenue
Atlanta, GA 30307

Rose Records
214 S. Wabash
Chicago, IL 60604

Val's Halla
723 1/2 South Blvd.
Oak Park, IL 60304

Dearborn Music
22000 Michigan Ave.
Dearborn, MI 48124

Schoolkid's Records
523 E. Liberty
Ann Arbor, MI 48104

Electric Fetus
2010 4th Ave. South
Minneapolis, MN 55404

**Tropicana Imports and
Music Center**
1314 East Lake St.
Minneapolis, MN 55407

Uhuru Books
1304 East Lake Street
Minneapolis, MN 55407

**World Beat Music
and Video**
1810 Riverside Ave
Minneapolis, MN 55454

Inside Africa
Galtier Plaza
175 E 5th St
St. Paul, MN 55101

Record Service
621 E. Green
Champaign, IL 61801

Record Swap
606 1/2 E. Green
Champaign, IL 61801

Hear's Music
2508 N Campbell
Tucson, AZ 85719

Bow Wow
3103 Central Ave.
Albuquerque, NM 87100

ABCD's
6406 N. IH-35 Suite 1301
Austin, TX 78752

Sound Exchange
2100A Guadalupe
Austin, TX 78705

Caravan Music
P.O. Box 49036
Austin, TX 78765
(Mail Order)

Waterloo
600A N. Lamar
Austin Tx 78703

VVV
3906 Cedar Springs
Dallas, TX 75219

Best Buy Chains
Dallas, Fort Worth

Wax Trax Records
626 E 13th Ave
Denver, CO 80203

Finest CD's and Tapes
1103 W. Elizabeth
Fort Collins, CO 80521

ABCD's
1119 W. Drake Rd.
Fort Collins, CO 80526

Aron's Records
1150 N. Highland Ave.
Los Angeles, CA 90038

Poo Bah Records
1101 E. Walnut
Pasadena, CA 91106

Rhino Records
1720 Westwood Blvd
Westwood, CA 90024

Trade Roots Records
2040 Fern Street
San Diego, CA 92107

Down Home Music
10341 San Pablo Avenue
El Cerrito, CA 94530
(retail & mail order)

Cymbaline
435 Front St.
Santa Cruz, CA 95060

Round World Music
593 Guerrero St.
San Francisco, CA 94110

Artichoke Music
3526 SE Hawthorne Blvd.
Portland, OR 97214

Music Millenium
3158 E. Burnside
Portland, OR 97214

Jump Jump Music
7005 NE Prescott
Portland, OR 97218

Backstage Music & Video
2232 NW Market Street
Seattle, WA 98107

Orpheum
618 Broadway East
Seattle, WA 98102

Wall of Sound
2237 2nd Ave
Seattle, WA 98121

Campus Music
2733 S. King St.
Honolulu, HI 96826

CANADA

Highlife Records & Music
1317 Commercial Dr.
Vancouver B.C. VSL 3XS

Black Swan
2936 W4th Ave.
Vancouver B.C. V6K 1R2

Hibicus
288 St Catherine St. West
Montreal

Le Rayon Laser
3656 Blvd. St. Laurent
Montreal

UNITED KINGDOM

**Stern's African Record
Centre**
116 Whitfield Street
London W1P 5RW
*Will play records for you; also have
a mail order service. Tube: Warren St.*

HMV
150 Oxford St. W1
London, England
*Also check other branches. Tube:
Oxford Circus*

Virgin Megastore
Oxford St. W1
Tube: Tottenham Court Rd

Africa Centre
38 King Street
London WC2E 8JT
Records, books, concerts,
bulletin board
*Tube: Covent Garden / Leicester
Square*

**Balham and Brixton mar-
kets**
South London
Good for highlife from Ghana

Blashara
47-49 Colston St
Bristol BS1 5BB

Decoy
30 Deansgate
Manchester M3 1RH

Jumbo Records
5/6 The Upper Mall
St John Centre
Leeds LS2 8LQ

Virgin Retail
131 Princess St
Edinburgh EH24 ATT

Tower Records
217 221 Argyle St
Glasgow G2 8DL

FRANCE

*Go to **FNAC:** several in Paris, just
ask. Main store is near Chatelet-
Les-Halles metro.*

Barbes Area
18th arrondissement, Paris
North African section of
city with many shops selling rai cassettes and videos.

Africassette
45 rue Doudeauville, 18th
Metro Chateau Rouge, Paris
Francophone west African cassettes

Virgin Megastore
52-60 Ave. des Champs
Elysees, Paris
Metro: Champs Elysees

Afric Music
3 rue des Plantes, 14th,
Paris
*African style. They'll play records
for you*

THE NETHERLANDS

Boudisque
Haringpakkerssteeg 10-18,
Amsterdam
Near Central Station

Fame Music
Kalverstraat 2, Amsterdam
Near Dam Square

Virgin Megastore
Nieuwezijds Voorburgwal
182, Amsterdam
Near Dam Square

SWEDEN

Afro Tropical
Drottning Gatan 110,
Stockholm

Multi Kulti
St Pauls gatan 3, Stockholm

El Barrio
Sodermanna gatan 10,
Stockholm

Chevere
Rorstrandsgatan 25,
Stockholm

GERMANY

Canzone
Savignypassage
S Bahn Bogen 583
1000 Berlin 12

FNAC Berlin
Meineckestr
Berlin 23

Scirocco
Ledererstr
19 Munich

Weltrecord
Eppendorfer Landstrasse 24
2000 Hamburg

FINLAND

Digelius Music
Laivurinrinne 2
SF 00120 Helsinki
(also does mail order)

ITALY

Pata Pata
Viale Corsica,
45 Milano
Ask for Bernard

SOUTH AFRICA

Reliable Radio & TV
316 Marshall Street
Jeppestown 2094
Johannesburg

City Music
Carlton Centre
Johannesburg

FESTIVAL INFORMATION

All festivals listed below have a healthy share of international artists. Advance hotel reservations recommended. Call or fax for information if you can. We urge you to support live music!

USA

Africa Fete
(throughout US) June-July
825 8th Avenue
New York, NY 10019
Tel: 212/603-3932

Reggae Sunsplash
(US, Japan, worldwide) June-July
115 West California Blvd., #177
Pasadena, CA 91105
Tel: 213/478-9487

New Orleans Jazz and Heritage Festival
last weekend in April, first in May
1205 N. Rampart Street
New Orleans, LA 70116
Tel: 504/522-4786

Festival Internationale de Louisianne
last weekend in April
P.O. Box 4008
Lafayette, LA 70502
Tel: 318/232-8086

Central Park SummerStage (free)
mid June through early August, Sunday afternoons are best for world music
(Rumsey Field in Central Park near 72nd St. on east side)
830 5th Avenue
New York, NY 10021
Tel: 212/360-2777 (office: 212/360-2756)

Celebrate Brooklyn (free)
Africa Mundo Festival (late July), other weekend concerts of interest throughout summer
Prospect Park Bandshell at 9th St.
Prospect Park in Brooklyn
Africa Mundo information:
303 Fifth Avenue, Room 1913
New York, NY 10016
212/685-8577

San Diego Street Scene
weekend after Labor Day
363 5th Avenue, Suite B110
San Diego, CA 92101
Tel: 619/557-8490
12 Blocks of music & food

Bumbershoot Festival
early September
Seattle, WA
Tel: 206/622-5123

Martinique Days
April weekend in New York
444 Madison Avenue, 16th floor
New York, NY 10022
Tel: 212/838-7800, ext 228

CANADA

Montreal Jazz Festival
about ten days in late June/early July
355 St. Catherine St.
W. Ste. 700
Montreal, Quebec H3B1A5

Summer Festival of Quebec (free)
first Thursday of July
120 St. Paul Street
C.P. 24, Station B
Quebec J1K7A1
Tel: 418/692-4540

Cultures Canada
July-August Various locations in National Capitol area
40 Elgin Street, Suite 202
Ottawa Ontario K1P1C7
Tel: 800/465-1867

Harborfront Centre Festivals
A Festival of World Roots Music June-August
410 Queens Quay West
Toronto Ontario M5MV2Z3
Tel: 416/973-3000

EUROPE

Musiques Métisses
end of May/beginning of June
BP 244
16007 ANGOULEME CEDEX
France
Tel: +33 45 954 342
Fax: +33 45 956 387

WOMAD Festivals
Summer, major travelling festival in UK, Canada, France, Finland, France, Japan
To be placed on mailing list write to
WOMAD Mailing List
Millside
Mill Lane, Box
Nr Corsham, Wiltshire SN13 8PN
ENGLAND
Regarding WOMAD in the US you can call:
Caren Campbell, 212/979-6269

World Roots Festival
mid-June
Melkweg Club
Lijnbaansgracht 234a
1017 PH Amsterdam
The Netherlands
Tel. +31 20 6248492
Fax +31 20 6201209

Heimatklänge Festival
July and August
Tempodrom
D-BERLIN
Germany
Tel + 49 30 313-4081
Fax + 49 30 313-1499
E-Mail PIRANHA@IPN-B.COMLINK.APC.ORG
Open air & free. Every year is a different musical theme

Sfinks Festival
late July
Patrick De Groote
J.F. Willemsstraat 10
B-2530 Boechout, BELGIUM
Tel: + 32-3-455-69-44
Open-air festival in a Victorian park near Antwerp

Afrika Festival
May 26-28
Würzburg, GERMANY
Tel. +49-933-880-100

Druga Godba Festival
June 10-17
Ljubljana, Slovenia
Bagdan Benigar
Tel. +386-61-13-17-039
Fax +386-61-322-570

World Music Festival
July
Rome, ITALY
Tel. +39-2-224-73-432

Kultodrom
September 1-3
Mistelbach, AUSTRIA
Tel. +43-2572-2292

M.E.L.A. Festival
several days starting around October France
Centre Jean Lurcat
24 rue Pierre Curie
F-33130, Begles
FRANCE
Tel. +33 56-85-80-05

AFRICOLOR
December 22-24
Théâtre Gérard Philipe
59 Blvd. Jules Guesde
93207 Saint-Denis near Paris
FRANCE
Tel. +33 147-97-69-99
Fax +33 1 47-97-65-44

**THE CARIBBEAN
AND AFRICA**

Reggae Sunsplash
early August
Montego Bay
Jamaica
212/567-2900

MASA
week in late April/early May
Market for African Performing Arts
Abidjan, Ivory Coast in West Africa
Booths for African performing companies, dozens of concerts from several African countries
Tel. 514/842-5866
Fax 514/843-3168

Certain times of year are especially good for live music in Africa. For example, Christmas in Dakar, Senegal is very lively. Ramadan in Islamic West African countries (one month in April/May, exact dates vary according to lunar calendar) is a slow time for live music. But just before or just after Ramadan is generally good.

SUGGESTED FURTHER READIING

PERIODICALS

Rhythm Music Magazine, monthly journal covering world music and global culture. Branching out to include art, dance, fashion and travel. 872 Mass Ave, 2-2. P.O., Box 391894, Cambridge, MA, USA 02139. 617-497-0356.

The Beat, longest running US publication featuring Caribbean, African, and world music. Extensive coverage of reggae. Published every two months by Bongo Productions, PO Box 65856, Los Angeles, CA USA, 90065.

Folk Roots Magazine, good features, reviews, and news on artists worldwide. Published on the penultimate Thursday of the month preceding cover date by Southern Rag Ltd., PO Box 3378, London N41TW England.

Stern's World Music Review: Tradewind, current information on new releases, record reviews, and world music news. Published monthly in London, available from Stern's African Music Centre, 116 Whitfield Street, London W1P 5RW, England.

Billboard, the international newsweekly of music, video and home entertainment that is continually expanding its worldwide coverage. World music and reggae charts every two weeks. P.O. Box 2011, Marion, Ohio, 43305, USA. 800-745-8922. (614-382-3322 from outside US)

Africa Report, excellent articles on African politics and society. Published six times a year by the African-American Institute. Subscription inquiries: Subscription Services, P.O. Box 3000, Dept. AR, Denville, NJ 07834.

The African News Weekly, news and commentary about Africa targeted to Africans living around the world. P.O. Box 242019, Charlotte, NC, 28224-2019, USA. 704-643-0909.

The African Times, bi-weekly paper of news and features on African politics, business, culture, and sports. 6363 Wilshire Blvd. Suite 306, Los Angeles, CA, 90048, USA. 213-951-0717.

N'dule Magazine, Afro-Paris news and gossip with emphasis on Zaire. 17, Boulevard Albert Camus, 95200 Sarcelles, France

BOOKS

Africa O-Ye! A Celebration of African Music by Graeme Ewens. Da Capo Press, 1992. Good history of contemporary African pop dealing with the continent by musical regions. Beautiful color photos. Pricey but worth owning. ISBN 0-306-80461-1

African Music: A Bibliographical Guide to the Traditional, Popular, Art, and Liturgical Musics of Sub-Saharan Africa by John Gray. Greenwood Press, 1991. Good resource book for further research. ISBN 0-313-27769-9

African Music: A Pan-African Annotated Bibliography by Carol Lems-Dworkin. Hans Zell Publishers, Oxford, England, 1991. Extensive bibliography, valuable for researchers. ISBN 0-905450-91-4

African Music: A People's Art by Francis Bebey. Lawrence Hill Books, Brooklyn, NY, 1975. Good overview of traditional African music featuring descriptions and photographs of instruments by Cameroonian musicologist and musician. ISBN 1-55652-128-6

African Musicology: Current Trends, Volume II ed. Jacqueline Cogdell Djedje. University of California Los Angeles, African Studies Association Press, 1992. Essays about African music and society by contemporary musicologists. ISBN 0-918456-62-2

African Rhythm and Sensibility by John Miller Chernoff. University of Chicago Press, 1979. Excellent book about African aesthetics and the traditional foundations of modern African pop. ISBN 0-226-10345-5

African Rock: The Pop Music Of A Continent, by Chris Stapleton and Chris May. Obelisk/Dutton, 1990. Good overall background book on contemporary African music. ISBN 0-525-48554-6

AFROPOP WORLDWIDE Listener's Guides co-edited by Sean Barlow and Ned Sublette. World Music Productions, five editions 1989-1993. Guest essays by Jon Pareles, Robert Palmer, Robert Farris Thompson, Banning Eyre and Gilberto Gil. Extensive discographies, maps and reference sections. See address on page IX.

ARChive Guide to World Music edited by Bob George and Richard Gehr. Random House/Pantheon, 1996. Encyclopedia of popular musics from non-western cultures.

Black Music of Two Worlds by John Storm Roberts. Original Music, 1982. Landmark book describing the connections between music of Africa, the Caribbean, and the Americas. ISBN 0-96144-580-7

Breakout: Profiles in African Rhythm by Gary Stewart. The University of Chicago Press, 1992. In-depth essays on key figures in African music. ISBN 0-226-77406-6

Congo Collossus: The Life and Legacy of Franco and OK Jazz by Graeme Ewings. Buku Press, 1994. Richly detailed, fascinating biography of the most influential composer, singer and bandleader in sub-Saharan Africa. ISBN 0-9523655-1-0

The World of African Music by Ronnie Graham. Pluto Press, 1992. Excellent reference book featuring extensive discographies and ethno-linguistic maps. ISBN 0-94839-003-4.

The Da Capo Guide to African Music by Ronnie Graham. Da Capo Press, 1988. Good historical reference book on country by country basis. Dated discographies, but valuable for listings of older recordings. See updated version above. ISBN 0-306-80325-9

Flash of the Spirit: African and Afro-American Arts and Philosophy by Robert Farris Thompson. Vintage, 1984. Inspired exploration of the African cultural diaspora. ISBN 0-394-72369-4

Hey You!: A Portrait of Youssou N'Dour by Jenny Cathcart. Fine Line Books, London, 1989. Informative biography of Senegalese and international star.

In Township Tonight: South Africa's Black City Music and Theatre by David B. Coplan. Longman, 1985. Fascinating social history of three centuries of black popular culture in South Africa. ISBN 0-582-64400-3

Juju: A Social History and Ethnography of an African Popular Music by Christopher Alan Waterman. University of Chicago Press, 1990. Engaging story of the roots and evolution of Nigeria's best known music. ISBN 0-226-87465-6. For maximum enjoyment also get the illustrative cassette. ISBN 0-226-87466-4

Makeba, My Story by Miriam Makeba with James Hall. New American Library, 1988. Moving account of Makeba's remarkable life, full of trials and triumphs. ISBN 0-453-00561-6

The Music of Africa by J.H. Kwabena Nketia. W.W. Norton & Company, 1974. Good introduction to traditional African music highlighting social and historical contexts. Transcriptions included. ISBN 0-393-09249

Musicmakers of West Africa by John Collins. Three Continents Press, 1985. Rare interviews with West African greats such as E.T. Mensah, plus essays on less well-known musicians. ISBN 0-89410-076-9

Nightsong by Velt Erlmann with an introduction by Joseph Shabalala. University of Chicago Press, 1995. Text on the South African Iscatamiya singing tradition popularized internationally by Ladysmith Black Mambazo.

The Rough Guide To World Music Edited by Simon Broughton, Mark Ellingham, David Muddyman and Richard Trillo. Rough Guides, 1994. 700 page handbook divided by regions including extensive sections on Africa. Targeted discographies. Features on stars and styles. Essential reference book. ISBN 1-85828-017-6.

The Soul of Mbira by Paul F. Berliner. University of California Press, 1978. Music and traditions of the Shona people of Zimbabwe. ISBN 0-520-04268-9

Three Kilos of Coffee an autobiography by Manu Dibango with Danielle Rouard. University of Chicago Press, 1994. Recounts the colorful life of Cameroonian maestro as he moves from one musical hot spot to the next. ISBN 0-226-14491-7

WORLD WIDE WEB SITES ON THE INTERNET:

http://www.npr.org/programs/afropop/ ....accompanies the National Public Radio series AFROPOP WORLDWIDE. Features APWW album of the week, program playlists, concert tour information, newsflashes, APWW photo- gallery, etc.

http://www.cityscape.co.uk/froots/ ....accompanies Folk Roots Magazine out of the U.K. Details contents of current issue, some reviews, charts, festival lists, onward connections to other web sites and news groups, etc.

ACKNOWLEDGEMENTS

The publisher would like to thank those who gave permission to reproduce the pictures listed on the copyright page, as well as the following people who contributed advice and assistance of various kinds: Donna Ruff for artwork; Emily Head for preparing the index; Rob Sugar from Auras Design for the map accompanying the introduction; Norman Sweeney of African Art Imports, New York; Frank Hanly. The publisher also thanks those listed below who helped the authors with information for the book, and joins **Jack Vartoogian** in thanking the people who helped to make his photography possible by providing access, support, and encouragement, including everyone at: The Apollo Theatre, The Bottom Line, Central Park SummerStage, Irving Plaza, Harambee and Kilimanjaro, Lincoln Center Out-of-Doors and Mid-Summers Night Swing, The New York Times, S.O.B.'s, Tramps and World Music Institute. The publisher has made every effort to ensure that the picture credits acknowledge the person or institution who holds the copyright to the images in the book; please notify the publisher if any errors have been made, so that these can be corrected in future editions.

The authors would like to thank all the African musicians who have shared their stories and their lives in countless interviews and performances. Their hospitality can never be repaid. Thanks to Sara Hunt of Saraband who persistently sought our involvement in this book project,

which she conceived and worked on with us. Thanks also to Marika Partridge who diligently edited all the copy in the text, drawing on her seven year involvement in editing AFROPOP and AFROPOP WORLDWIDE on National Public Radio.

Special thanks to the following reviewers who added information and insights to this book based on years of experience and research: Rob Allingham for South Africa; Werner Graebner for East Africa; Gary Stewart and Ken Braun for Congo/Zaire; Andy Frankel for Nigeria; Georges Collinet and Benedict Nkeng for Cameroon; Charles Easmon for Ghana; Ramiro Mendes for Cape Verde and Angola; Randy Barnwell and Bill Lawrence of Ishtikara Music for northern Africa; and Maria Golia for Egypt. Thanks to the many individuals at the following record companies for putting out the music and helping us track down albums and photos: Stern's Africa; Mango, Rounder, Shanachie, Rykodisc, Buda, Blue Silver, Africassette, Original Music, Lyrichord, Caroline Records, RealWorld, GlobeStyle, World Circuit, Xenophile, Sonodisc, Piranha, Popular African Music, Gallo, and Tusk.

Thanks to Georges Collinet, the host of AFROPOP WORLDWIDE from NPR and the most enjoyable radio partner imaginable, for sharing his stories and insights on African music from the '60s to the present. Thanks to all the co-producers of AFROPOP WORLDWIDE on NPR who have contributed reportage on Africa over the years:

Rob Allingham, Werner Graebner, Markus James, Banning Eyre, Ellen Barlow, Ofebea Quist-Arcton, Lanre Adjayi, John Collins, Femi Solowah, Danny Zwerdling, Henry Kaiser, Maria Golia, Ned Sublette, Georges Collinet, James Eoppolo, Randy Barnwell, Bill Lawrence, Andy Warshaw, Charles Easmon, Debbie Williams, and Carolyne Swinburne.

Sean Barlow thanks his first teachers, Abraham Adzenyah and Freeman Donkor. Thanks also to Ibrahim Kanja Bah of the African Music Gallery and Leo Sarkisian of the V.O.A. for early advice and encouragement. He thanks Carol Dorsey for encouraging him as a writer. Eternal thanks also to the Corporation for Public Broadcasting, National Public Radio, the National Endowment for the Arts and the Rockefeller Foundation for believing in and supporting research for the AFROPOP radio series, especially to Rick Madden, La 'Verne Washington, Sandra Rattley-Lewis, Peter Pennekamp, Alberta Arthurs, Ellen Buchwalter, Stephen Lavine, Suzanne Sato and Joan Shigekawa. Thanks to the enthusiastic, hardworking team at National Public Radio and to all the wonderful people in public radio across the U.S. who like to dance and know good music when they hear it.

Banning Eyre would like to thank all of the African musicians he has had the pleasure and privilege to play with and learn from, as well as Phyllis Rose and V.S. Naipaul for their inspiration, advice and support in his early years as a writer.

INDEX